TEACH
TO
SELL

TEACH TO SELL

Why Top Salespeople *Never Sell* –and What They Do Instead

DAN ROCHON

SAVIO REPVBLIC

A SAVIO REPUBLIC BOOK
An Imprint of Post Hill Press
ISBN: 979-8-89565-306-7
ISBN (eBook): 979-8-89565-307-4

Teach to Sell:
Why Top Salespeople Never Sell—and What They Do Instead
© 2026 by Dan Rochon
All Rights Reserved

Cover Design by Jim Villaflores

posthillpress.com
New York • Nashville
Published in the United States of America

1 2 3 4 5 6 7 8 9 10

Dear Small Businessperson, Salesperson, and
Entrepreneur,

This book is dedicated to you.

You started this journey chasing freedom and
prosperity—only to find out it's tough as hell.

Maybe you're just starting and trying to figure
things out. Or maybe you've had a killer sales
month…followed by crickets. Maybe the money's flowing, but your time isn't yours anymore.

Yet, you keep going—because that's who you
are. Determined. In control of your future.

**So how do you create No Broke Months
without working yourself into the ground?**

Keep reading. You'll find out.

Table of Contents

Introduction

I'M GUESSING THAT YOU BOUGHT this book because you are struggling to figure out where your next sale will come from, or you're currently at a standstill in your business and don't know what to do next.

Maybe you're worried that if things don't change soon, bills won't get paid, and your family's needs won't be met.

Or perhaps the thought of going back to a nine-to-five job or starting over in another career makes your stomach turn.

Here's the truth: If you spend more time trying to figure out how to make sales than actually selling, you're on the fast track to running out of cash.

This book will show you how to change that—so you can sell more, stress less, and never worry about another broke month.

WHO WILL BENEFIT FROM READING THIS BOOK?

This book is for:

- The hungry newcomer trying to land their first deal
- The seasoned pro looking to break through the plateau
- The top producer who wants to scale their success

Sales isn't about luck—it's about process. And you're about to master it.

> This book is specifically crafted for:
>
> - Small business owners
> - Sales professionals
> - Entrepreneurs
>
> It addresses the universal need for sales skills to achieve success.
>
> Recognizing the essential role sales plays in the journey of every businessperson and entrepreneur, I will collectively refer to all three groups throughout the book as:
>
> - Salespeople

HOW WILL YOU LEARN FROM USING THIS BOOK?

Visit www.NoBrokeMonths.com/TeachToSell to download the worksheets that accompany this book. These resources will help you apply the lessons, take action, and create real results.

Each chapter follows a structured approach to ensure your success:

- **Relatable Story**—A real-life example to illustrate the topic
- **Pre-Decision Compass**—A tool to help guide your thinking before you apply the concept
- **Key Concepts**—Clear explanations of what you need to know

- ***Teach to Sell Exercise***—Learn how the methodology applies to the topic and how to use it in real-world sales.
- **Chapter Summary**—A recap to reinforce what you've learned
- **Commit or Quit Challenge**—A push to take action and implement the lessons

This structure ensures that you're not just reading—you're learning, applying, and growing.

WHAT MAKES THIS BOOK DIFFERENT?

Teach to Sell isn't another sales book. It's a step-by-step system designed to make you unstoppable. It will show you:

- **Proven frameworks** that work in any industry
- **How to sell AND elevate yourself in all areas of life**
- **Tactics that come from real-world sales—not just ideas**

This isn't fluff. It's decades of success and failure, boiled down to a formula you can follow.

WHY DID I WRITE THIS BOOK?

I have been in business and sales for most of my life and have gained immense experience. During the journey, I had, unfortunately, witnessed hundreds (and thousands) of people failing in business—a true shame.

A few years ago, I faced a major setback and had to sell the large real estate brokerage I had owned for over a decade.

Have you ever taken a step back, feeling frustrated, only to realize later that it allowed you to move forward, no longer held back? That was my experience.

During that time, I felt uncertain about my next move. So, I reached out to the most influential person in sales for guidance. I made a commitment to myself that if he agreed to mentor me, I would follow his advice to the letter.

He agreed to mentor me based on one condition. He asked me to write this book to tell all the steps I learned and share them with others.

After many years of learning the sales business, I wrote the blueprint you now hold in your hands.

I invested my time, knowledge, and money into writing this book because being a salesperson has helped me live the life I want, and I am passionate about helping you do the same.

WHERE DID I LEARN WHAT YOU WILL READ?

Over the past twenty years, I've researched and studied the habits of over five hundred successful entrepreneurs to uncover their secrets to success. I've started, owned, bought, and sold multiple businesses along the way.

It took more than two decades to learn sales and persuasion techniques and nearly as long to master them in sales, forming this book's foundation.

This book shares the wealth of knowledge I've accumulated, presenting it in a captivating and easy-to-understand format.

Throughout my career, I've traveled the country, attending hundreds of seminars and workshops, always hungry for knowledge.

I've stood onstage as a keynote speaker, presenting to hundreds of audiences—**and with each one, I've gained just as much insight as I've shared.**

In addition, I have paid an estimated over $1M for coaches to guide me (and another $1M for those I have led).

I have trained in the specialty area of neuro-linguistic programming and hypnosis. But don't worry—I'm not going to try to make you cluck like a chicken (unless you are into that sort of thing). Instead, strategies will be explained to create desire and urgency, helping others to decide.

The pages that follow condense much of this knowledge.

When you study this guide, you will learn what I learned (without investing the time and money that I did).

HOW IS THIS BOOK UNIQUE?

Teach to Sell stands out from other sales books. It provides specific systems and processes for success and helps you become the best version of yourself. To be the best salesperson, you could choose to excel in all areas of life.

Decades of learning, failing, and succeeding in sales have been documented and explained in the lessons that will be poured for you.

The more you study this guide, the more obvious it will become that you will achieve success. The truth of how to succeed in sales is right in front of you.

TEACH TO SELL APPLICATION—WHY DO SO MANY PEOPLE FAIL?

Sometimes people go into business for the wrong reasons.

They falsely believe they can make easy money, and lots of it.

Average salespeople earn about $60,000 a year, and sales are one of the hardest (not Alaskan crab boat fisherman hard, but emotionally hard) professions worldwide.

Yet the top performers make six and seven figures. Why? Mastery of the craft.

Here's the hard data:

- Only **28 percent of sales professionals** expect to hit quota. (Burdett, 2024)
- Around **44 percent of salespeople** quit after just one follow-up, but **80 percent of sales** require at least five touches. (Sales Stats, Quota and On-Boarding, 2023)
- Just **29 percent of sales professionals** consistently close deals. (Storm, July)

Without the right skills, most salespeople will continue to struggle. This book fixes that.

PRE-DECISION COMPASS

How can you effectively anticipate and prepare for difficult decisions in your personal and professional life?

You can choose to make the most critical choices before the moment of decision arrives.

Imagine having a reliable guide in your pocket, ready to help you make the best decisions, even before the moment arrives.

With the Pre-Decision Compass, you will learn a simple yet powerful method to anticipate your choices. When these difficult situations happen, this compass will remind you of the decision you've already made, helping you stay true to your values and goals.

SUMMARY: WHAT IS YOUR PRIORITY IN SALES?

Business exists to create clients. If you're uncomfortable seeking out clients, you're limiting your potential.

This book will teach you how to *Teach to Sell*, so you never have another broke month again.

COMMIT OR QUIT CHALLENGE: WILL YOU DO THE WORK?

This book isn't just theory—it's an action plan. Throughout, you'll find **Teach to Sell Exercises**. You can skip them or do them. The choice is yours.

Your challenge: **Commit to applying what you read.** Skip steps, and you'll struggle. Engage fully, and you'll win.

FINAL THOUGHT—WILL THIS BOOK CHANGE YOUR LIFE?

That's up to you. My team and I have made millions using these strategies. The following pages will show you how.

To your success!

Dan Rochon,
Clifton, VA
March 2026

Part I

BELIEVE IN YOURSELF

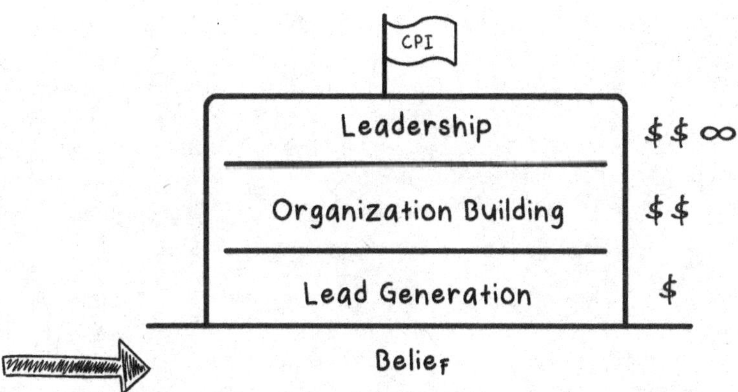

CHAPTER 1

What Does It Mean to
Teach to Sell?

A STORY OF TRUST AND TRANSFORMATION

Imagine being a ten-year-old kid whose world had just fallen apart.

Your dad left, and your mom, who had always been there for you, had to start over. She worked during the day to pay the bills and trained in the evenings to become an X-ray technician.

You were a latchkey kid, no guardian at home.

You endured brutal beatings from your older brother that left you paralyzed with fear.

If someone had been your friend, they might have visited you in a roach-infested apartment across the Oak Park Mall in Overland Park, Kansas.

Your lunch was most often a peanut butter sandwich—jelly was too expensive of a luxury.

Times were tough for that child.

That kid was me.

Then, Mr. Kasper came into my life.

He was my sixth-grade teacher, and he cared. He showed me I was worthy, and that belief helped me through those hard times.

It's been over forty years, but if Mr. Kasper walked into my life today and offered advice or asked something of me, I'd follow him without question.

Mr. K earned my trust back then.

THE POWER OF A GREAT TEACHER

Do you remember your favorite teacher, coach or guide?

Think back.

Who was your number one?

What grade were you in?

What made them special?

It likely was more than teaching subjects like algebra, history, or English.

They helped you solve a problem or reach a goal. Maybe they listened when you struggled with your self-image or a bad breakup.

They cared.

Imagine your trusted teacher appeared today.

Would you take their advice?

I bet you would.

Why?

Because they earned your trust.

Mr. Kasper taught me, and your favorite teacher taught you. They earned our trust.

The example above illustrates the concept of *Teach to Sell*.

THE CORE OF *TEACH TO SELL*

What Is *Teach to Sell*?

As you might imagine, businesses live and die on sales.

And if you really want to sell, you must understand that it's not about you. It's about understanding the other person's perspective.

> *Teach to Sell* is a way to build trust and gain influence by showing another how to think so they can get what they want, which will help them feel inspired to follow your lead.

Sales thrive on trust.

And how do you build trust?

Through mastery.

That's where *Teach to Sell* comes in. Teaching someone shows them you know what you are talking about, which leads to sales.

Teach to Sell is the ONLY system that ensures **No Broke Months**.

You build deep trust by guiding your clients and showing them the true value of what you offer. This trust turns into loyal customers, more sales, and a steady, abundant income.

When you embrace *Teach to Sell*, you will transform your business and have financial freedom and success.

Applying the tactics and strategies in this book will prevent predictable transaction problems, sparing you from constantly reacting and spending your days putting out fires.

When you teach your clients what to expect, you create a vision they can see and feel.

PRE-DECISION COMPASS: *TEACH TO SELL* BY SERVING, NOT SELLING

Before applying *Teach to Sell*, ask yourself:

- What problem does my customer need to solve?
- How can I educate them in a way that empowers them?
- What objections do they have, and how can I teach them through it instead of trying to convince them?
- Am I speaking their language or just pushing my product?

THE LADDER OF TRUST

Am I speaking their language
or just pushing my product?

What objections do they have,
and how can I teach them through it?

How can I educate them
in a way that empowers them?

What problem does my
customer need to solve?

By answering these questions, you ensure you are building trust instead of just making a pitch.

PRE-DECISION TO MAKE

You can **Pre-Decide** that before every sales conversation, you will shift your focus from selling to serving.

Instead of pushing a product, you will commit to understanding your customer's problem, educating them with value, and guiding them through objections with trust—not pressure.

By doing this, you position yourself as a trusted advisor, not just another salesperson.

TEACH TO SELL IN ACTION

How Do You Build Trust Through Teaching?

Studies show that when you feel supported, you become more capable, in control, and deeply connected.

Researchers at Harvard University have examined the role of communication in building trust and agree that *Teach to Sell* works. (Smith & Brown, 2020)

Their foundational research reveals how support fosters capability, control, and connection, leading to trust and enduring relationships.

How Does *Teach to Sell* Work in Business?

When you want something, you often grab an app and order the product or service you want using companies like Amazon, Netflix, or Uber Eats.

Today, the consumer rarely relies on a salesperson when buying.

To thrive in a world ruled by billion-dollar giants, businesses must shift from selling to teaching.

Adopting a *Teach to Sell* approach builds loyalty and increases the likelihood that consumers will engage with and follow your business, giving you a competitive edge.

What Are Examples of Companies Using *Teach to Sell*?

Patagonia

Patagonia, an outdoor clothing company known for its commitment to environmental activism, exemplifies the *Teach to Sell* approach through its campaigns.

Instead of focusing solely on products, Patagonia educates its audience through documentaries, blogs, and social media, envisioning a future where responsible consumer choices and environmental concerns intersect.

This strategy builds trust by aligning with customers' values, portraying Patagonia as a clothing brand and a leader in environmental stewardship.

HubSpot

HubSpot, a marketing and sales platform, drives sales through education by offering free, valuable resources. These include blogs, e-books, webinars, and online courses that teach businesses effective marketing, sales, and customer service strategies.

By educating its audience and providing practical resources, HubSpot builds trust and establishes itself as an industry authority, attracting and retaining loyal customers.

Both Patagonia and HubSpot successfully blend education with their sales approach, creating a deeper connection with their customers and fostering long-term loyalty.

How Important Is Understanding the Customer's Experience in Driving Successful Sales?

Teach to Sell is about gaining influence by establishing your authority and expertise. It is teaching others to gain their trust.

When you share valuable insights and proven strategies, you don't just teach—you inspire. You become a trusted leader, guiding clients to see your credibility and the true value of what you offer.

With *Teach to Sell*, you don't just gain trust; you create a following that believes in you.

THE NUMBER ONE SALES MISTAKE
What Gets in the Way of *Teach to Sell*?

Salespeople often face various challenges due to common mistakes, including:

- Talking too much instead of listening to the customer
- Failing to understand the customer's needs and offering irrelevant solutions
- Overpromising and underdelivering, which can damage trust
- Skipping follow-ups after initial contact
- Not qualifying leads early, wasting time on unlikely prospects
- Ignoring objections rather than addressing them directly
- Focusing on price instead of the value offered
- Neglecting to build rapport before pitching products or services

What Gets in the Way of Teach to Sell?

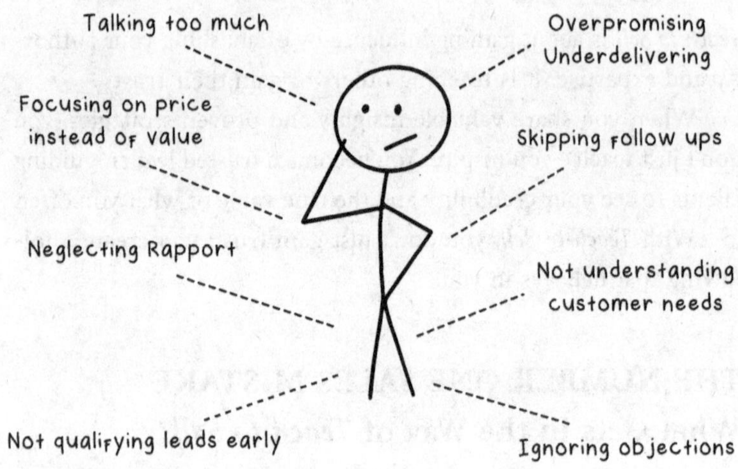

However, none of these is the top mistake.

What Is the Number One Sales Mistake?

The biggest obstacle to successfully implementing *Teach to Sell* is the pervasive feeling of being "not good enough."

Throughout this book, you'll see a recurring theme that holds most people back from reaching their goals: self-doubt.

You might think your sales process isn't good enough, your website isn't good enough, or, worst of all, *you* aren't good enough.

It's easy to think negatively, especially when juggling multiple tasks.

You might believe a potential client won't buy because your service could be better or because you doubt your capabilities. This self-doubt can manifest in several ways, holding you back from achieving your sales goals:

Self-Doubt: Lacking confidence can prevent you from even starting the sales process, stopping you from reaching out to potential clients.

Unclear Sales Process: Without a clear roadmap, you might feel like you're wandering through a maze, unsure of each step. This uncertainty can make you feel inadequate and stuck.

Multitasking Overload: Taking on too many tasks at once can be overwhelming. You might feel like you're not good enough to handle everything, leading to a lack of focus and productivity.

Negative Assumptions: Prejudging a prospect's interest, thinking they'll never buy because you're not good enough or your product isn't perfect, can lead to missed opportunities.

All-or-Nothing Thinking: The pressure to close every deal can be daunting. If you don't see immediate success, you might feel discouraged and think you're not good enough to succeed in sales.

Procrastination: Delaying important activities like prospecting or following-up can stall your progress. You might procrastinate because you feel you're not good enough to get the desired results.

Lack of Guidance: Without proper training or coaching, you might struggle to refine your skills, making you feel like you're not good enough to excel in sales.

Limited Support Network: Feeling isolated can make your sales journey even more challenging. You might feel like you're not good enough without a supportive team cheering you on.

Giving Up Easily: Persistence is crucial in sales. You might be tempted to quit too soon because you feel you're not good enough to achieve the success you desire.

Recognizing these obstacles is the first step in overcoming them.

Remember, the belief that you're "not good enough" is just a mindset, and you can change it.

Consider the story of Candy Lightner, the founder of Mothers Against Drunk Driving (MADD).

In 1980, Lightner's thirteen-year-old daughter, Cari, was tragically killed by a drunk driver.

This devastating loss spurred Lightner into action. She created MADD to advocate for stricter drunk driving laws and raise public awareness about the dangers of driving under the influence.

Lightner faced immense internal pain and external resistance.

Many doubted her, seeing only a grieving mother, not an activist who could change the law.

Yet, she persevered, drawing national attention to drunk driving issues.

As MADD grew, Lightner encountered internal conflicts and was eventually removed as president. Despite this, her efforts led to over seven hundred new laws, including raising the drinking age to twenty-one, and enforcing tougher penalties for drunk driving. Lightner's work saved countless lives and transformed public attitudes. (McCarthy, 2003)

You might face doubts and a lack of support, with people questioning your sales efforts and urging you to find a stable job.

This lack of encouragement can be disheartening but remember Lightner's story. Her persistence led to monumental change, and your determination can lead to success, no matter what the obstacles.

Overcoming the "not good enough" mindset requires action, guidance, and support. This book will provide you with clear directions and actionable steps to improve your sales efforts and build your confidence.

Remember, it's not about being perfect. It's about taking the first step, learning, and growing. This book is here to guide you, help you navigate the challenges, and remind you that you are good enough.

What Holds Us Back from Achieving Our Goals?

Often, it's our fears and doubts.

Thinking about fears and doubts reminds me of a trip to a beautiful resort in Punta Cana when my daughter, Maggie, was about five. It was a magical place where performers from Cirque du Soleil practiced and put on incredible shows for us.

Maggie met a trainer who encouraged her to try the flying trapeze. She was so excited, even though it was a bit scary.

She put on a safety harness and started climbing the tall ladder step by step. But as she got higher, fear took over, and she climbed back down.

When she reached the ground, I leaned in close, my voice filled with warmth and encouragement, as I spoke softly to lift her spirits.

Maggie took a deep breath, gathered all her courage, and started climbing again. This time, she made it to the top. She jumped forward, and suddenly, she was flying through the air, her laughter echoing above the safety net below.

It was breathtaking. When Maggie landed back on the ground, I asked her, "Sweetie, how did that feel?"

She looked up at me, her eyes wide, and said, "Daddy, I was scared."

I smiled and said, "And you did it anyway. How do you feel now?"

With pride and excitement, Maggie beamed, "I feel great, Daddy!"

I hugged her and told her, "We all feel fear sometimes. You can live in fear or faith but not both."

In that moment, Maggie learned courage isn't the absence of fear; it's choosing faith and moving forward despite it.

COMMITMENT FUELS RESILIENCE: THE BOUNCE BACK FROM REJECTION

Sales are often a rollercoaster. You'll experience the joy of closing deals and the crushing blows of rejection. Without a deep commitment to your goals, discouragement can easily lead to quitting.

Consider the story of Howard Schultz, the former CEO of Starbucks.

When Schultz first tried to convince investors of his vision for a national chain of coffeehouses, he faced numerous rejections. Many thought his idea would fail. But his unwavering commitment to his vision strengthened his resilience.

He transformed Starbucks into a global coffee empire through relentless effort and innovation. By 2024, Starbucks had over thirty-eight thousand stores worldwide, a testament to Schultz's commitment in the face of immense challenges. (Howard Schultz: The Man Behind Starbucks' Success, 2018)

COMMITMENT BREEDS FOCUS: SHARPENING YOUR SALES SWORD

Sales require multiple tasks: prospecting, lead nurturing, presentations, and follow-ups. Half-hearted efforts can quickly scatter your focus and lead to missed opportunities.

Michael Jordan, regarded as the best basketball player of all time, is a legend for his laser focus. Despite his immense talent, Jordan's unwavering commitment to constant practice and self-improvement set him apart.

He practiced relentlessly, honing his skills and refining his game. This dedication to focused effort translated into on-court dominance, securing six NBA championships for his teams.

COMMITMENT UNLOCKS CONTINUOUS IMPROVEMENT: THE LIFELONG LEARNER

Sales is a field that demands constant learning and adaptation. A committed salesperson actively seeks to improve their skills and refine their strategies.

Oprah Winfrey, a titan of the media industry, didn't achieve her success overnight. Even after becoming a household name, Oprah remained dedicated to learning and growing.

She actively sought out mentors, participated in workshops, and constantly pushed herself to reach new heights. This lifelong commitment to self-improvement fueled her continued success for decades.

LEARNING FROM FAILURE: EMBRACING THE INEVITABLE MISS

The idea of "committing to failure" might seem counterintuitive, but it's crucial in the context of sales. Rejection and missed deals are inevitable.

Committing to learn from these failures is where the true magic happens.

Steve Jobs, the visionary co-founder of Apple, is known for his groundbreaking innovations.

However, his journey wasn't without its setbacks. He was famously ousted from Apple in the early 1990s. Instead of viewing this as a failure, Jobs used it as a learning experience. He went on to co-found NeXT and Pixar, both highly successful companies. (Steve Jobs, 2011)

These experiences ultimately fueled his return to Apple, where he led the development of iconic products like the iPod and iPhone.

Remember, success in sales isn't guaranteed.

But by committing fully, you equip yourself with the resilience, focus, and drive necessary to navigate the challenges and ultimately achieve your goals.

Like Schultz, Jordan, Winfrey, and Jobs, your commitment becomes the foundation for a successful sales career.

TEACH TO SELL EXERCISE: EDUCATE TO CONVERT

Scenario: You're selling a high-end service or product. How can you educate a potential client before they ever interact with you?

List three common pain points of your ideal customer.

____

____

____

Write down a teaching-based solution for each pain point (not a pitch).

____

____

____

What type of free resource (blog, video, checklist) could you create around one of these topics?

____

This exercise shifts your mindset from "closing the sale" to "guiding the customer," leading to increased trust and conversions.

CHAPTER SUMMARY: WHAT DOES IT MEAN TO *TEACH TO SELL?*

At its core, *Teach to Sell* is about building trust. Think back to a teacher who changed your life—the one who believed in you, guided you, and made an impact.

That trust they built with you is the same foundation that *Teach to Sell* brings into business and sales.

Key Takeaways

- **Sales is not about you; it's about your customer.** People buy from those they trust, and trust is built through teaching and providing value.
- **Selling is teaching.** When you educate your audience, you position yourself as the expert, making them more likely to follow your advice.
- **Trust is everything.** Your customers must believe in you before they believe in your product.
- **The companies that win don't just sell—they educate.**
  - Patagonia builds trust by aligning with customers' values through environmental activism.
  - HubSpot generates sales by offering free educational resources like blogs, webinars, and courses.

The #1 Mistake That Holds Salespeople Back

The biggest roadblock in sales isn't external—it's internal.

- The "not good enough" mindset is the silent killer of success.
- Self-doubt leads to:
  - Hesitation in making sales calls
  - Fear of rejection and failure
  - Overthinking instead of taking action
- The key to overcoming this? Commitment to action, learning, and persistence.

Success Comes from Commitment

The most successful people weren't free from fear—they pushed through it.

- **Howard Schultz (Starbucks)**: Rejected multiple times before turning Starbucks into a global brand.
- **Michael Jordan:** Cut from his high school basketball team but relentlessly practiced until he became the best.
- **Oprah Winfrey:** Faced early career setbacks but never stopped growing, learning, and evolving.
- **Steve Jobs:** Fired from his own company, but used failure as a learning experience to return stronger.

Their success didn't come from talent alone—it came from commitment.

Commit or Quit Challenge: Your Choice— Your Transformation Begins

Right now, you are standing at a crossroads. Life feels familiar, but something is missing.

Maybe you're experiencing inconsistent sales, self-doubt, or the frustration of working hard without predictable results. You know you're capable of more, but you're stuck in the same cycle.

Then comes the moment of truth—the realization that something must change.

You can continue down the traditional sales path, where trust is fragile, transactions are unpredictable, and your income fluctuates month to month.

Or—you can take the leap into *Teach to Sell*, where trust becomes your greatest asset, sales become effortless, and **No Broke Months** become your new normal.

- Imagine clients seeking you out because they trust your expertise.
- Picture closing deals with ease—not through pressure, but through education and value.
- Visualize a life of financial freedom and consistent success—all because you chose to teach instead of sell.

The biggest roadblock isn't your skills, your market, or even your competition—it's the belief that you're not good enough.

Most people let doubt hold them back. But the truth is, success isn't about talent—it's about commitment.

Right now, you have a choice.

Stay where you are, or step into the transformation that will change everything.

Your journey starts now.

Will you Commit or Quit?

CHAPTER 2

Transform Before You Can
Teach to Sell

A DEFINING MOMENT: THE BEGINNING OF THE JOURNEY

It was New Year's Day, 1987. I was a thirteen-year-old boy. I didn't recognize how the previous years of abuse affected me. I had no role model.

My older brother still beat the shit out of me every day. My mother believed we were just boys "being boys," and I had no safe place to go.

By the time I had my sixth swollen black eye, and my front tooth lay shattered on the concrete from another brutal blow, the truth finally sank in—this wasn't normal. This wasn't how life was supposed to be.

That New Year's Day, I stumbled upon something that would change everything. My brother had left a six-pack of Bud Light in the trunk of his rust orange 1972 Chevrolet Chevelle, parked in our garage.

Four warm beers later, I was laid flat on my back on the unused weight bench. My mind was spinning, and I vomited all the contents of my stomach onto the floor.

That day marked the beginning of my drinking career. I had no idea it was also the first step in numbing a deep, unshakable sense of unworthiness.

THE BATTLE WITHIN: OVERCOMING THE MENTAL PRISON

Before you can *Teach to Sell*, you must first teach yourself to overcome your own barriers.

It took decades before I finally realized how deeply I had been trapped in the false belief that I was not enough.

The feeling of inadequacy lingered throughout my life, buried within my subconscious, surfacing at the most inconvenient moments.

A few years back, I found myself in Seattle, Washington, attending a small, exclusive real estate conference. The room was filled with some of the country's top agents, each exuding confidence and success.

As I sat among them, a storm of doubt began brewing.

Every conversation I overheard seemed to amplify my insecurities. Their achievements felt like towering mountains beside my modest hills.

The more I listened, the more I felt like an imposter.

My heart started to race, my breathing became shallow, and a sense of dread crept over me. I could feel the walls closing in, the air growing thicker, making it harder to think, harder to breathe.

Panic surged through me, a tidal wave of anxiety crashing over my sense of reason.

My mind screamed at me that I didn't belong, that I was a fraud who had somehow slipped into a world I had no right to be in.

I felt trapped, desperate to escape the weight of my own self-judgment.

This is the same mental prison many people experience in sales. Doubt, comparison, and fear of rejection keep them from stepping into their potential.

In a frantic bid to regain some sense of control, I cut my trip short and asked my assistant to book me an early flight home.

Sitting in the terminal, waiting to leave the city and the crushing pressure behind, I couldn't shake the feeling of failure.

Looking back, I see how I was unfairly measuring myself against the best. Instead of seeing it as an opportunity to learn and grow, I allowed my doubts to overshadow my accomplishments and potential.

That panic attack was a stark reminder that I am vulnerable.

THE TURNING POINT: LEARNING TO BOUNCE BACK FASTER

Another instance that deeply affected me was when I applied to refinance my townhome to pay my payroll because I was in a jam.

It turned out that an assistant had signed up for utilities at a property we managed out of state without my knowledge but failed to pay the $148 electric bill.

This mistake damaged my credit, preventing me from securing the loan I desperately needed.

The frustration left me feeling deeply inadequate.

It weighed heavily on me, casting a shadow over my financial plans and causing immense stress during an already challenging time.

When setbacks happen, the key to success is not avoiding failure, but mastering the skill of bouncing back faster.

Another time I recall was when an employee who worked for me left the company, taking one of our largest accounts with them.

The client's choice to follow him made me question my worth as if they saw my former employee as more capable than me.

I was consumed by the belief that I wasn't good enough, that I had let my team and myself down. And the sense of betrayal from this incident upset me.

Sales and business aren't just about transactions. They are about relationships, trust, and self-perception.

The weight of these thoughts was suffocating, and the relentless inner turmoil left me feeling utterly defeated.

Maybe you can relate.

Think about when something made you feel like you didn't measure up.

What happened?

Consider a time when you found yourself comparing yourself to someone else, making a mistake, or feeling betrayed.

Do you remember how you felt?

Perhaps you felt inadequate, frustrated, or hurt. Those emotions were intense and consuming, making you question your worth and capabilities.

You may have felt stuck in a cycle of negative thoughts, unable to see a way forward. The experience might have left you feeling isolated and disheartened as if you were alone in your struggles.

However, those challenging moments have also shaped you and built resilience. They have prepared you for what lies ahead.

The first step to mastering *Teach to Sell* is transforming your mindset. If you don't believe in yourself, how can you expect others to believe in you?

Like the journey that thirteen-year-old boy had in front of him, you will have to face your battles and feelings for whatever stops you.

The stakes are high—your sense of self hangs in the balance; this is a quest for your worth, a challenge pushing you beyond your limits, demanding everything you have.

Your old beliefs, the ones that whisper,

"I'm not good enough, I'm not smart enough."

These are the dragons you must slay. Each step you take will be a step toward discovering that you are and always have been worthy.

Your ordinary world is about to change. The journey will be challenging, with trials and dark moments when you might want to give up.

But remember, this is a matter of life and death. The life of your true self, waiting to be claimed, and the death of the old, limiting beliefs that have held you captive.

The path is before you. Take that first step, and let's uncover your worth together.

PRE-DECISION COMPASS: REWRITING THE NARRATIVE OF YOUR SUCCESS

Reflect on past experiences where you felt unworthy, incapable, or stuck. What false narratives have shaped your beliefs about yourself and your abilities? Recognizing these patterns is the first step toward transforming them.

Ask yourself:

- When have I doubted myself and why?
- How have these doubts impacted my actions and decisions?
- What evidence do I have that contradicts these beliefs?
- What would happen if I chose to believe in my own success?

PRE-DECISION TO MAKE

You can **Pre-Decide** that when old, limiting beliefs surface, you will recognize them for what they are—lies that no longer serve you. Instead of letting them define you, you will consciously choose to embrace the truth: you are capable, worthy, and unstoppable.

BELIEF STARTS HERE—ELIMINATE THE UNKNOWN IN SALES

Do you recall the feelings you experienced when you left home to begin your adult life?

Remember that first night on your own as an adult, venturing into the unknown?

Can you feel the mix of emotions bubbling within you?

It is like standing at the edge of a cliff, uncertain where your next step will take you but ready to leap.

Being a salesperson can be very unsettling, like the experiences described above.

We never know whether our actions today will produce the desired results, and we seldom have certainty about the outcome of our decisions. Consequently, we are often uncomfortable about the future, especially when it feels like we must take big risks to achieve big rewards.

This uncertainty amplifies our fears, making it even harder to stay optimistic about what lies ahead.

So, how can you easily navigate the unknown?

For many years, I taught entrepreneurs to believe in themselves.

However, I realized that this advice was too vague.

Instead, you should believe in your ability to figure things out. This mindset shift can empower you to take on challenges with confidence.

Another powerful tool you can use comes from neuro-linguistic programming (more on that later), which is known as the "as-if" frame.

WHAT IS THE "AS-IF" FRAME?

The "as-if" frame involves acting as if you are already the person who has achieved the results you desire. By doing so, you start embodying the qualities and actions of that successful person, which helps you achieve those outcomes and attain what that person has for yourself.

This approach can transform your mindset and behavior, aligning you more closely with your goals.

WHAT DO SALESPEOPLE COMMONLY EXPERIENCE WHEN THEY DO NOT KNOW THE FUTURE?

You got into business to gain money and freedom. But then you realized how hard it is to be a businessperson.

Anxiety is a common emotion that arises from the unpredictable potential threats that may occur in the future.

In the realm of sales, it is crucial to believe in success and our ability to steer our lives and shape the outcomes of events.

> Success hinges on the power of belief.

WHAT HOLDS YOU BACK—AND HOW TO OVERCOME IT

The Elephant Rope Story: Breaking Free from Limiting Beliefs

Imagine a baby elephant tied to a stake with a strong rope.

At first, the little elephant tries with all its might to break free, but the rope holds tight. As the elephant grows bigger and stronger, it could easily break the rope, but something stops it.

Years of believing it can't escape have made it think it's stuck forever.

Just like that elephant, people sometimes have beliefs that hold them back.

These beliefs start when we're young or because of things that happened to us before. They can make us feel like we can't do things, even when we're strong enough to try.

But just as the elephant can learn to break free, we can learn to change our beliefs. We can believe in ourselves and try new things.

We don't have to feel stuck like the elephant.

It is essential to challenge limiting beliefs because they can hold you back from reaching your full potential and achieving your goals.

Limiting beliefs are negative thoughts or assumptions about yourself or the world around you, which can create self-doubt, fear, and anxiety. They can also prevent you from taking risks or trying new things, limiting your personal and professional growth.

Challenge limiting beliefs to replace negative thoughts with positive ones. This builds confidence, resilience, and a growth mindset, leading to success and fulfillment in life and work.

For example, if you believe you need to be better to succeed in your business, you may avoid taking risks or pursuing new opportunities.

However, if you challenge this belief and replace it with a more positive and empowering view, such as "I have the skills and knowledge to succeed in my career," you may feel more confident and motivated to take on new challenges and achieve your goals.

Challenging limiting beliefs can help you overcome self-doubt and fear, build resilience and confidence, and achieve remarkable success and fulfillment in your personal and professional life.

Common False Beliefs That Hold People Back

The roadblocks (lies/false beliefs) that get in many people's ways include thoughts such as:

- I am not worthy.
- I am not good enough/smart enough.
- It takes too much time/money.
- I am too busy.
- I am too young/old.
- I have too many other responsibilities.
- I start things and do not finish them.
- I cannot do it/It can't be done in my market.
- It is too risky.

You could use the previous list to help you know what thoughts might be holding you back.

But What If Confidence in Yourself Is Still Lacking?

In such cases, you can employ a clever maneuver to fabricate belief, even if your self-assurance is currently wavering. The details of this strategy are outlined in the following section.

TAKE ULTIMATE RESPONSIBILITY

Have you ever been in the office or at an online meeting and overheard a water cooler conversation about the many reasons another is struggling?

They always say things like:

"The other person didn't return my call."

"I don't have adequate support or training."

"My client doesn't care about me."

The litany of complaints seems endless. However, dwelling on grievances about your perceived circumstances only makes you feel worse.

What can you do instead of focusing on your circumstances that do not serve you?

Take ultimate responsibility!

You can either believe that life "happens" to you or take charge of your existence.

What Is Ultimate Responsibility?

Ultimate responsibility means recognizing that EVERYTHING in your life results from your creation; this doesn't mean that you are to blame for everything that happens, but it does mean that you are accountable for it.

> You can have reason or results.
> You can't have both.

When you accept ultimate responsibility, you will seek solutions instead of reasons.

Example: Overcoming Financial Pressure

Many years ago, a big deal I was counting on suddenly fell through. The person who was supposed to buy something from me lost their job, and everything crashed.

My team needed to be paid the next day, and I needed the money from the deal that did not close to pay them.

I sat at home, listening to the joyful sounds of my wife and daughter playing in the next room.

But inside, I was overwhelmed.

The bills loomed over me like a mountain, making it hard to catch my breath. My stomach churned with pain, like a storm swirling inside me.

It felt like a weight was bearing on me, tightening around my neck.

My vision narrowed to my trembling hands, damp with sweat despite feeling frozen. Fear paralyzed me, like being trapped in quicksand, unable to move.

So, I called my bank and asked for a loan.

Luckily, they knew me well because they were from our town. And guess what? They said yes.

Disaster avoided!

Was it my fault the buyer lost his job?

No way!

But it was my responsibility to find a solution to the problem.

HOW CAN YOU EASILY GAIN FAITH IN YOUR FUTURE?

It can be frustrating if you have not reached your goals or just started in sales.

To believe in yourself, you can study others who have been where you are and seek success models of those who have overcome similar obstacles to break free from limiting beliefs.

When I started in sales, I studied models of success and derived **Blind Faith** from those who were successful before me.

If you have yet to succeed, you could emulate other successful people's actions. Acting while being committed (not attached) to the outcome can help.

Studying others carefully and replicating their behavior as closely as possible gets higher and quicker results, leading to the fast obtainment of **Absolute Faith**.

Think of other people who look like you, have a similar background, and have had success. What actions did they take? How can you duplicate those actions?

CAN YOU SUCCEED IN SALES?

You can do this! Your mind is infinite, and you will find the answers. Choose to do well.

Your thoughts, beliefs, attitudes, and experiences will define your existence.

If struggling, rest assured that the answer to what holds you back exists—BELIEVE IN YOURSELF!

And if you are still struggling, you have my permission to borrow my belief in you because the fact that you are reading this demonstrates to me that you are worthy of my belief!

WHY DO YOU DO WHAT YOU DO?

When I first entered the world of sales, my motivation stemmed from a deep desire to escape the grind of waiting tables. The thought of going back to that life if I failed in sales fueled my determination.

Over the years, my perspective has shifted, but my passion remains authentic.

You can enhance your skills through learning and practice. You might have a lower ability in an area. Yet, if your motivation is high and you have a mindset full of energy, you can choose to work hard to compensate for any skill deficiency.

Some people take pride in making sales to make a lot of money. While having money or power is not a bad thing (when used properly), it will massively restrict you if it is your predominant motivation.

When challenges arise, money alone will not sustain you. Profound purpose drives more tremendous success.

Think of the *Teach to Sell* exercises like a brain workout!

Just a quick burst of effort can unlock hidden potential and sharpen your skills. Ready to feel that post-workout accomplishment?

Do the exercise and reap the rewards!

TEACH TO SELL EXERCISE: UNCOVERING YOUR TRUE SALES MOTIVATION

In the following exercise, be candid in your responses. Please be "real" when you answer the questions below. Instead of being altruistic, state why you sell today.

Never having to drive an Uber to pay your bills is closer to your answer than bringing fresh drinking water to countries in need.

You may find yourself in sales to cover rent, manage alimony payments, or own your dream car.

Whatever your driving force, embrace it with raw honesty.

FIND YOUR DEEPEST "WHY"

Why are you in sales?

____

____

____

____

What is important to you about that?

____

____

____

____

Keep asking yourself, "What is important to me about that?" until you reach a core answer that fuels your drive. Write down:

"I make sales to ________, so that ________"

Post this on your desk as a daily reminder.

WHY DO I DO WHAT I DO?

I make sales to help others achieve their goals, so that they can be, do, and have more.

My mission is to help others achieve their goals through my writing, speaking, and coaching. That is part of the reason I wrote this book. I knew that both you and I could be, do, and have more.

TEACH TO SELL EXERCISE: CHALLENGE YOUR LIMITING BELIEFS

Identify the Limiting Belief: Write down a belief that might be holding you back. (Example: "I'm not good enough to succeed in sales.")

____

____

____

Gather Evidence: Find proof that both supports and contradicts this belief. Look at past achievements or examples of others who have succeeded.

____

____

____

____

Evaluate the Evidence: Objectively assess whether your belief is based on facts or unfounded fears.

Replace the Belief: Rewrite it into a positive statement. (Example: "I have the skills and knowledge to succeed.")

Take Action: Start operating as if your new belief is already true.

TEACH TO SELL EXERCISE: DEFINE YOUR MOTIVATION

Who is someone in your field with a similar background who has succeeded?

What specific actions did they take?

____

____

____

____

How can you replicate their steps?

____

____

____

____

CHAPTER SUMMARY: TRANSFORM BEFORE YOU CAN *TEACH TO SELL*

Before you can effectively *Teach to Sell*, you must first transform yourself.

This chapter explores the deep-seated beliefs that hold us back, the moments that shape our sense of worth, and the mindset shifts necessary to break free from limiting patterns.

Key Takeaways

- **Transformation begins with self-awareness.** Many of us carry hidden beliefs of inadequacy, often stemming from past experiences. Recognizing these false narratives is the first step to breaking free.
- **Your past does not define you—your response to it does.** The pain of childhood, moments of failure, or feel-

ings of betrayal are not who you are. You have the power to rewrite your story.

- **Fear and doubt manifest in business and sales.** Panic attacks, imposter syndrome, financial setbacks, and betrayal can trigger feelings of being "not good enough." These challenges are not signs to quit but signs to grow.
- **The greatest battle in sales is not external—it's internal.** Your success is determined by how you handle uncertainty, setbacks, and limiting beliefs. Your ability to navigate the unknown and develop confidence will define your path.

Breaking Free from Limiting Beliefs

The Elephant Rope Story: Like a baby elephant that grows strong enough to break free but still believes it's trapped, we often live under limiting beliefs from our past.

Common false beliefs that hold people back:

- I'm not worthy.
- I'm not smart enough.
- It's too risky.
- I don't have enough time/money/resources.
- Success is for others, not me.

Rewriting Your Story: By challenging these thoughts, you step into your full potential.

Building Faith in Yourself

The "As-If" Frame: Acting as Your Future Self

Instead of "believing in yourself," believe in your ability to figure things out.

Use the "As-If" Frame: Act *as if* you are already the successful version of yourself. This reprograms your brain to align with your future success.

Study Success Models

Look at people who started where you are and achieved what you want. Copy their mindset, actions, and strategies.

Taking Ultimate Responsibility

You can't control everything, but you are responsible for finding solutions. Life doesn't "happen" to you—you *create* it. Instead of focusing on circumstances, focus on actions.

Example: When a major deal fell through, I had to find a solution to pay my team. Taking ownership and seeking a way forward made all the difference.

The Power of Purpose Over Money

Money alone won't sustain you in difficult times. True motivation comes from something deeper:

- Providing value
- Helping others succeed
- Becoming the best version of yourself

Sales is not just about making money—it's about creating impact.

Commit or Quit Challenge: Success Demands Action, Not Excuses

Face your fear. Identify one major limiting belief and commit to rewriting it today. Stop letting it define your future.

Find a model of success. Choose one person in your field who has overcome a similar challenge. Learn what they did and commit to applying one of their strategies.

Write your why. Clearly define why you are in sales and what drives you.

Write it down and place it somewhere visible.

Take immediate action. Do one thing today that aligns with your transformed mindset. Whether it's making that difficult sales call, attending a networking event, or setting a bold new goal—act now.

Transformation isn't something that happens overnight. But the decision to commit to it happens in an instant.

Will you Commit or Quit?

CHAPTER 3

Wherever You Are, Make a Start

THE MOMENT EVERYTHING CHANGED

In my late twenties and early thirties, I worked as a waiter at the highest-end steakhouse in Washington, DC.

Senators, lobbyists, and celebrities would meet there to win over and impress each other. They dined on eighty-five-dollar dry-aged porterhouse steaks and drank bottles of Bordeaux wine that cost more than $350.

After 9 p.m., the back-dining area would become congested with the light blue fog of cigar smoke. I would overhear conversations that would be broadcast in the breaking news section of *The Washington Post* the next day.

On those rare slow days, we would glance at the televisions hanging above the giant wrought-iron eagle that guarded the kitchen entryway and watch the talking heads spit insults as if they were main characters in the Hatfield–McCoy conflict. The previous night, those same combatants had cordially dined together at the same table.

I earned a lot of money, but I hated my job.

I knew I wanted more. I dreamed of owning a business, helping people reach their goals, and building something of my own. But I had no idea how to make it happen.

I met with business brokers, attended franchise fairs, and had lunch with owners of businesses who intended to sell.

My efforts created no real opportunities. I continued to search.

The only clear conclusion this amounted to was that I did not have nearly enough money to start a business.

I pleaded with relatives to loan me the money that was needed. Their reception was less than warm—they told me to go to a bank.

So, I did. I walked into a bank, hoping for a loan, only to hear one word I had never given much thought to before: **collateral**. The bankers wanted security before handing over a quarter to half a million dollars. Imagine that—banks wanting a guarantee before lending money!

I felt stuck. I wanted to build something of my own, to create a future, to help others. But every attempt to secure funding ended in rejection. No assets. No mentors. No direction. Just a relentless drive to escape the life I had come to hate.

I pursued countless opportunities that left me more confused than ever.

Then, I came across a lesson that shifted my thinking entirely, one that exemplifies the *Teach to Sell* methodology: **When you simplify your focus, eliminate distractions, and commit to a clear path, success becomes inevitable.**

I realized my biggest problem wasn't a lack of opportunity—it was my scattered focus. I had been stretching my energy in too many directions, chasing too many possibilities. Until I gained clarity, I would continue to struggle.

It wasn't just a revelation for me; it became the foundation of how I now help others. *Teach to Sell* is about cutting through the noise, leading people to clarity, and empowering them to take decisive action.

I was beginning to understand that success isn't about waiting for the perfect moment—it's about creating it. My path was in front of me.

PRE-DECISION COMPASS: THE POWER OF FOCUS AND ACTION

Success doesn't come from talent alone; it comes from committing to the path, even when obstacles arise. Wherever you are today, your starting point is exactly where you need to be. The only thing that matters is making the decision to move forward.

Take a moment to reflect on the roadblocks—both real and imagined—that have held you back. What patterns have kept you from making progress?

The first step to breaking free is recognizing the false narratives that have shaped your beliefs.

Ask yourself:

- What distractions have kept me from making real progress? Have I been chasing too many goals at once instead of committing to what truly matters?
- Where have I hesitated, and why? Have I let fear, doubt, or lack of clarity stop me from taking action?
- What moments in my past prove I am capable? Have I overcome obstacles before? Do I have wins—big or small—that show I can succeed?

- What would change if I committed fully to my top priority? If I focused on one goal with relentless dedication, how different would my results be?

PRE-DECISION TO MAKE

You can **Pre-Decide** that from this moment forward, distractions will no longer derail you. When limiting beliefs or competing priorities arise, you will:

- Recognize distractions as obstacles to your real goals.
- Prioritize only what truly matters and say no to everything else.
- Replace hesitation with action and commitment.

Success isn't about waiting for the perfect moment—it's about choosing the right focus and taking decisive action. Your path is already in front of you. The only question is: Are you ready to commit?

SET YOUR GOALS AND FOCUS ON ACHIEVING THEM

There is a story about Warren Buffett and his long-time pilot, Mike Flint. Flint had an established career as a pilot, which included flying Air Force One and medivac for the Air Force, as well as working as Buffett's private pilot. (McNicholas, 2013)

One day, Buffett told him,

> "The fact that you're still working for me tells
> me I'm not doing my job. You should be out,
> going after more of your goals and dreams."

Buffett then asked Flint to write down his top twenty-five goals. Once Flint did, Buffett instructed,

"Now circle your top five goals."

Then Buffett gave the most crucial advice,

> "Avoid the other twenty goals at all costs until you have achieved one of the five." (Richards, 2018)

That lesson resonated with me. I realized that my problem wasn't a lack of ambition—it was a lack of focus.

I was trying to chase every opportunity, but in doing so, I was making no real progress. I needed to choose a path and fully commit.

During a Q&A session at Apple's Worldwide Developers Conference (WWDC) in 1997, Steve Jobs said,

> "People think focus means saying yes to what you've got to focus on. But that's not what it means at all. It means saying no to the hundred other good ideas that there are."

I finally understood: It wasn't just about working hard—it was about working smart. I needed to prioritize the right goals, block out distractions, and take focused action toward what truly mattered.

This is the core of the *Teach to Sell* method—when you master how to think, eliminate confusion, and align your actions with your goals, you can guide others to do the same.

By teaching others to prioritize, simplify, and commit, you inspire them to take charge of their own success. This is how you create influence—not by pushing, but by guiding them toward clarity and action.

Be selective. Prioritize only what truly matters.

HOW WILL YOU GET THERE?

If you live in Toledo, OH, and try to drive to Tallahassee, FL, using backroads without a GPS or map, it's unlikely you'll reach your desired destination.

However, if you make the same journey with the help of Waze or a GPS, you can be confident that you'll arrive successfully.

To ensure you reach your destination, we'll use the following GPS framework:

1. One <u>Goal</u>
2. Three <u>Pathways</u>
3. Five <u>Steps</u> to reach the end of each pathway.

HOW DO YOU USE THE GPS FRAMEWORK IN BUSINESS?

The GPS framework establishes a specific goal, subsequently dissected into three key pathways with five steps to reach the end of each pathway.

The goal and path should be quantifiable targets, ensuring a precise measure of success, whereas the steps function as detailed plans designed to realize the end of each pathway.

You will meet the ultimate benchmark for goal achievement when you reach the end of all three pathways.

HOW DO YOU IDENTIFY THE RIGHT GOALS?

For your goals, consider how you can help the clients you serve.

1. What do you enjoy doing?
2. What does the market need from your product or service?
3. What is the most incredible thing you could achieve by helping your client?

I coach the owner of a company that makes e-commerce brands go viral on social media. He regularly gets millions of views for his clients.

Recently, my client shared a key takeaway from a class I taught: The money you make is proportional to the problem you solve.

When creating content for his clients, he focuses not only on hooking the viewer and being entertaining, but also on sharing valuable information and educating his client's audience. In other words, he embraces the strategy of *Teach to Sell*.

His goals include having at least three pieces of content go viral per client each month. Achieving this goal allows him to leverage the success into more business for himself.

As you develop your goals, remember the above strategy.

GPS Framework

Write 1 Goal

Close **20** Deals per Month!!!

Write 3 Pathways

Optimize
Lead Generation

Enhance
Client
Relationships

Improve
Sales Techniques

Write 5 Steps to Reach the End of Each Pathway

- Identify Target Market

- Utilize Online Marketing

- Build a Strong
  Online Presence

- Network and Collaborate

- Implement Referral
  Programs

- Provide Exceptional
  Customer Service

- Stay in Touch Regularly

- Offer Valuable Market
  Insight

- Personalize Your Approach

- Follow Up after
  Transactions

- Master Product Knowledge

- Hone Negotiation Skills

- Utilize Sales Script

- Practice Roleplay
  and Scripts

- Learn to Listen for
  Motivation

GPS Framework

Write 1 Goal

Write 3 Pathways

Write 5 Steps to Reach the End of Each Pathway

Repeat the task on the previous page five times, focusing on one of your five goals. Doing so will create a comprehensive blueprint to guide you to achieve **No Broke Months**.

- Your Goals to your Vision
- Your Pathways to your Strategic Routes
- Your Steps to your Mission

WHEN WILL YOU DO THE WORK?

You have established your sales compass by grasping the purpose behind your actions. With five chosen goals and a clear GPS route, it is time for you to decide when to embark on the journey toward achieving those goals.

You have heard of the concept of time blocking and understand its benefits, yet you might grapple with the implementation.

Weekly Calendar

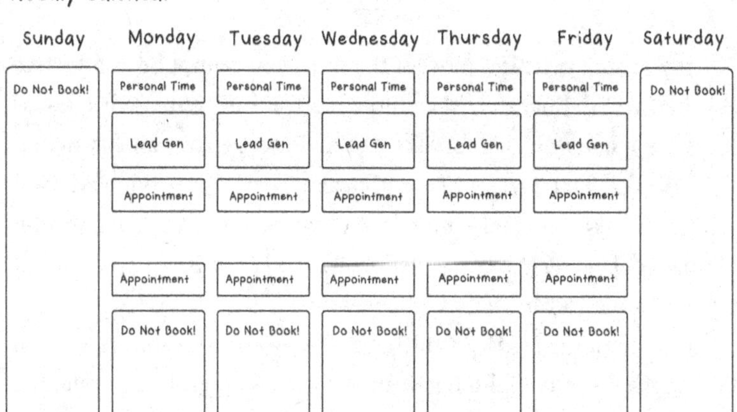

HOW DO THE TOP SALESPEOPLE BLOCK THEIR TIME?

Prioritize your personal commitments before dedicating time to crucial work activities.

WHAT IS THE QUICKEST WAY TO SUCCEED IN SALES?

To advance your career further, faster, and better, taking the time to think and plan is essential. Starting in sales involves constant work, with seldom any time taken off to plan or think.

> Winning happens before the game starts.

If you stay in action most of the time, you cannot be as effective as when you deliberately take time off. You can return with colossal force when you take breaks to unwind, prepare, and evaluate.

On *The Tim Ferriss Show* podcast, Ferriss interviewed Paul Levesque, aka thirteen-time WWE wrestling world champion "Triple H." During the conversation, Triple H recalled a story about a professional boxer, Floyd Mayweather. (Ferriss, 2015)

On September 19, 2009, at the MGM Grand Arena in Las Vegas for the fight between Mayweather and Juan Manuel Márquez, Triple H visited Mayweather in his locker room before the bout.

He found Mayweather lying on a couch watching a basketball game. Puzzled, Triple H asked Mayweather if he was wound up about the fight that would begin in minutes.

"Why would I be wound up?"

Mayweather replied.

"I'm either ready, or I'm not. Worrying about it right now ain't gonna change a damn thing. Right? Whatever's gonna happen is gonna happen. So, I've either done everything I can to be ready for this, or I have not."

Triple H nodded in agreement, and they enjoyed the basketball game on TV before the upcoming fight.

Mayweather took the time before the match to rejuvenate, preparing himself mentally for the impending challenge. Fueled by passion and thorough preparation, he emerged victorious with a unanimous decision.

HOW DO YOU USE MAYWEATHER'S STRATEGY TO BECOME A CHAMPION?

To best receive results, be sure you have done the exercises above, outlined your goals, and created five GPS routes for optimal results.

You will now take substantial, focused action by accomplishing the necessary Steps of the Pathway on your journey toward those Goals.

However, before finalizing your schedule, follow Mayweather's example and plan for designated time off because the purpose of a business is to serve you—not to be your master.

You will achieve more exceptional results when you plan with enthusiasm and take regular time off. Then, like Floyd Mayweather, you will be prepared to compete when it is time to perform. You've either done everything you can to be ready, or you have not.

WHAT ARE THE MOST CRITICAL PRIORITIES IN SALES?

In your sales business, the top priority is generating leads. Without leads, there's no business to close.

In sales, the critical tasks that drive results are:

Consistent and Predictable Income (CPI) Time (Working in Your Business)

1. Lead generation
2. Convert the leads for an appointment
3. Attend the appointment to get hired
4. Negotiate
5. Scripts and roleplay

Leveraged Time (Working on Your Business)

1. Recruiting talented people to your team
2. Selecting the right people to be in business with
3. Training those people to reach their goals
4. Leading those people to know how to think to reach their goals
5. Motivating those people to reach their goals

Self-Time (Working on Yourself)

1. Manage the money
2. Planning
3. Take planned rest and breaks

While the pivotal tasks in your business might vary slightly from those mentioned above, your objective is to prioritize anything that will yield the optimal outcome. However, always prioritize lead generation as the foremost focus.

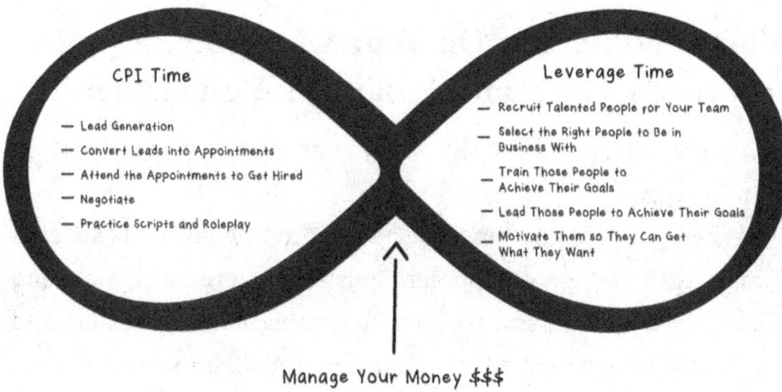

SCHEDULE THE ACTIONS OF YOUR PATHWAY.

If Staying on Task Is Challenging for You, What Should You Do?

Consider this approach if, like so many others, you find it challenging to dedicate chunks of your day to a singular task.

> Knock out the important stuff early.
> Then, you will have more energy and
> be able to remain focused.

Begin by reserving a brief period at the start of your morning for your most crucial job. Mastering the art of one to three focused hours each day is your initial triumph—your gateway to enhanced productivity.

When Should You Do Your CPI Time, Leveraged Time, and Financial Management?

Tackle the most critical tasks when your energy is at its peak in the morning.

When you take the time to generate leads, convert those leads to meet with you, go on appointments to get hired, negotiate and practice your scripts, and roleplay first thing in the morning, and you handled the essentials, you'll breeze through the rest of your day, meetings, and routine tasks with finesse, leaving time to browse social media (come on, we all need a little break).

Why Is Locking in Your CPI Time First Thing a Game-Changer?

Science backs it up—your brain is at its sharpest in the morning.

Research in chronobiology (yeah, we're getting fancy) shows that cognitive function and alertness peak shortly after waking, during what's called the "peak of circadian arousal." (Schmidt, 2007)

Studies on productivity highlight the importance of tackling high-priority tasks early in the day.

This approach, akin to "eating the frog first," leverages higher energy and willpower levels in the morning, leading to more significant task completion and overall productivity. (Tracy, 2011)

While not a specific study, insights from sales psychology suggest that decision-makers are more receptive and less tired earlier in the day. This optimal timing can increase the likelihood of successful lead-generation efforts and negotiations. (Adams, 2018)

It's not just about getting things done; it's about doing them when you're at your peak.

What Do You Do About All the Other Stuff that Takes Up Your Time?

Delegate less crucial tasks to others for help.

Right now, as I write this, the lawn care professional is outside, handling the mowing. By outsourcing tasks like lawn maintenance, I can stay locked in on what truly matters—writing (which happens to be one of the highest priorities of an author).

The same principle applies to your business. Delegate tasks that don't fall under **CPI Time, Leveraged Time,** or **Self-Time,** whether it's house cleaning, admin work, or anything that pulls you away from high-value activities. Freeing yourself from low-impact tasks means more focus on what moves the needle.

What Do You Do About All the People in Your Life Who Distract You from Your Business?

Amidst the pandemic, I made my daughter, Maggie, a commitment with her home for school and me working remotely.

I assured her that every lunch, from noon to 1:00 p.m., and every evening until 6:00 p.m., would be exclusively ours. I held true to this promise, and like clockwork, at 11:59 a.m., Maggie stood outside the office door to ensure the commitment was kept.

In return for these dedicated moments, understanding was requested during focused business hours from 8:30 a.m. to noon and from 1:00 p.m. to 6:00 p.m. Remarkably, she complied.

The crucial lesson here is that honoring this promise means earning the privilege of concentrating on business tasks. Consequently, countless lunches were shared, engrossed in board games and laughter. The gains extended far beyond business priorities because what mattered most was prioritized initially.

Communicate the importance of maintaining focus to those around you, seeking their understanding and support.

Clearly delineate when you are available, minimizing the chances of unwarranted interruptions. Your success hinges on this deliberate approach to preparation.

How Do You Manage the Other Distractions?

To effectively manage distractions, eliminate the myriad interruptions disrupting modern life. Quiet the constant pings of social media alerts on your phone and free yourself from the non-stop buzz of ringtones and text notifications.

Research from the University of California underscores this approach, revealing that individuals who reduce their frequency of social media checks tend to experience lower stress levels and higher productivity. (Maclay, 2018)

Similarly, a study conducted at the University of British Columbia advocates managing emails in batches—either as a morning routine or during an end-of-day session. This practice maintains a clutter-free inbox and preserves mental clarity for more critical tasks. (Chapman Learning Commons, 2024)

By addressing emails at the periphery of your day—before diving into productive activities in the morning or wrapping up in the evening—you can ensure a pristine inbox that won't obstruct your path to focused work.

This strategic approach minimizes distractions and maximizes productivity, fostering a conducive environment for achieving your goals.

But What About Client Care?

You may have noticed that you haven't yet prioritized taking great care of your clients.

Undoubtedly, surpassing your client's expectations is the heart and soul of crafting an outstanding business.

By prioritizing **CPI Time**, **Leveraged Time**, and **Self-Time** activities, you lay the foundation to genuinely cater to your clients' needs effectively.

Your efforts should be to exceed your client' expectations. To be successful in sales, you must have this mindset.

Every year, Amazon's Jeff Bezos hosts the Machine learning, Automation, Robotics and Space (MARS) event. At his event, he shared that a business owner or salesperson should be a missionary, not a mercenary.

He said,

> "Entrepreneurs who champion their clients'
> interests always end up making more money…
> they always win." (Datoo, 2019)

If the strategy of obsessing over your clients works for Bezos, you might consider doing the same. As you continue reading, think about how you can over-deliver the steps.

AS A BUSINESSPERSON, HOW COULD YOU ADD A BENEFIT TO YOUR CLIENTS?

As dedicated salespeople or business professionals, our mission is multi-faceted in supporting our clients.

We go beyond mere transactions; we share our wealth of wisdom and knowledge, providing reassurance and expert guidance at every step.

Our commitment is to surpass the expectations of our clients. This entire book is a testament to the value we consistently bring to those we serve. It is more than a profession; it's a dedication to elevating experiences and forging lasting relationships.

TEACH TO SELL EXERCISE: STRATEGIC GOAL EXECUTION

After identifying your top goals, define three pathways to achieve each goal, and write each of those below the goal.

What particular actions will you undertake to navigate through your chosen pathway successfully? As you elaborate on the following, consider:

- Your values
- Who will be instrumental in helping you?
- How will you approach and treat those individuals who contribute to your goal attainment and others along the way?

Goal (1): Write one of the five goals from the above exercise.

Pathways (3): Transition to measurable priorities aligned with your business streams. When achieved, these targets will propel you toward your overarching goal.

1. Pathway 1: _______________________________
2. Pathway 2: _______________________________
3. Pathway 3: _______________________________

Write five steps for each Pathway you selected.

Your steps are the lifeblood of your plan, representing commitments to yourself and crucial areas of accountability. Stimulate your thinking by asking,

"What steps must I take to reach the end of
the pathway?"

As you apply this exercise, remember that *Teach to Sell* is about more than just achieving your own goals; it's about guiding others to do the same. The clearer and more structured your approach, the easier it will be to help others follow your lead.

TEACH TO SELL EXERCISE: ELIMINATING DISTRACTIONS

Who usually distracts you from work? How can you allocate time for them so they respect your business hours?

____

____

____

____

A top salesperson on my team solved this by getting a separate phone just for work, free from social media distractions. Studies show reducing social media checks lowers stress and boosts productivity. Implement similar tactics to stay focused.

Teaching others to recognize and eliminate distractions is part of the *Teach to Sell* philosophy—it's about helping them create an environment where they can thrive.

TEACH TO SELL EXERCISE: OVER-DELIVERING FOR CLIENTS

Bezos said:

> "Don't satisfy your customers. Figure out how to delight them. That is the number one thing. Whoever your customers are." (Datoo, 2019)

Sales is about exceeding the expectations of others. How can you add unexpected value to clients?

____

____

____

____

Think beyond transactions; educate, reassure, and guide them at every step.

The *Teach to Sell* method is about guiding people to what they truly need, rather than just giving them what they ask for. By becoming a trusted authority, you build lasting relationships and a thriving business.

CHAPTER SUMMARY: WHEREVER YOU ARE, MAKE A START

No matter where you are in life or business, your next step is what truly matters.

My journey from waiting tables at an elite DC steakhouse to building a thriving business wasn't fueled by luck, it was powered by focus, persistence, and a willingness to start where I was.

Key Takeaways

- **Success isn't about endless effort, it's about focused effort.** Warren Buffett's "Top 5 Goals" method teaches that prioritization is the key to achieving what truly matters.
- **Set clear goals and follow a structured path.** Using the **GPS framework** (One Goal, Three Pathways, Five Steps), you create a roadmap to predictable success.
- **Time management is everything.** Elite performers, like Floyd Mayweather, focus on preparation and execution while eliminating unnecessary distractions.
- **Lead generation is the #1 priority in sales.** Everything else supports this core activity.
- **Customer obsession wins.** As Jeff Bezos said, "Entrepreneurs who champion their clients' interests always end up making more money...they always win."

Your success starts with clear priorities, disciplined execution, and eliminating distractions.

Commit or Quit Challenge: Focused Action or Endless Distraction

You have two options:

1. **Continue as you are**—juggling too many goals, allowing distractions to consume your time, and struggling with inconsistent results.
2. **Choose *Teach to Sell*,** focus on what truly matters, and take committed action toward success.

Success isn't about being busy, it's about being intentional. *Teach to Sell* is about demonstrating how to think, not just what to do. When you lead others through this process, you empower them to create their own success.

When you commit to mastering *Teach to Sell*, refining your focus, and eliminating distractions, success is inevitable.

So, will you keep chasing every opportunity and staying stuck, or will you take control, simplify your path, and step into a future of **Consistent and Predictable Income**?

Commit to focused action or stay lost in distractions. **The choice is yours.**

Will you Commit or Quit?

CHAPTER 4

Your Path to Success

FROM ROCK BOTTOM TO REINVENTION

I was thirty-two years old.

At the time, I was what you might call a functioning alcoholic. But looking back, it would have been better if I had been non-functioning. Maybe I would have made different choices sooner.

Each morning, I woke up dehydrated, my head pounding. As pain throbbed behind my eyes, I whispered a familiar lie:

"I will not drink today. I will not drink today. I will not drink today."

I chugged water, forced myself through a shower, and headed to the posh DC steakhouse for the 10:30 a.m. shift meeting.

Hours of being hungover later, the cycle of drinking repeated itself. By 7:00 p.m., I felt human again. By 10:00 p.m., I took the first sip of beer or wine, and by sunrise, I had downed a twelve-pack and two bottles of wine before passing out; only to wake up and do it all over again.

Then came the final crash.

I woke up on the bathroom floor of a three-bedroom townhome in Alexandria, VA—dry heaving, my kidneys screaming, my skull splitting. Hours passed in the fetal position, waiting for the agony to subside.

That day, something broke. Amidst the tears and despair, a flash of clarity emerged: *There has to be more than this.* But fear gripped me. Alcohol had been my comfort, my escape, my identity. Who was I without it?

Then I thought of my best friend, Dave.

Dave never told me to quit drinking. He just shared his truth—his struggle, his triumph. He showed me that change was possible.

His example became my turning point.

That day, I chose sobriety.

Rehab followed. The withdrawals were horrific—a suffering I never want to relive. But on the other side was something I hadn't known in years: clarity.

For the first time, I committed—not just to quitting alcohol, but to a new way of being. Sobriety became my most prized possession, the foundation upon which I rebuilt my life.

Emotionally, I had been stuck at sixteen, reckless and impulsive. But sobriety accelerated my growth. I shifted from *"have to"* to *"choose to,"* stepping beyond my comfort zone and redefining what was possible.

That shift led me to reconsider my dreams. I had always wanted to be a business owner. Real estate emerged as a promising path.

It was late 2007, headlines screamed *foreclosures, worst economy ever, government bailout.* Fear whispered that I had no experience, no business stepping into this field. But I enrolled in pre-licensing school anyway.

The sixty-hour course cost $2,000—peanuts compared to other ventures. The potential, however, was limitless. Effort in meant reward out. For the first time, I saw a way forward.

Despite stepping into a new venture with no experience and fearing judgment, the path to entrepreneurship was clear.

As I entered the industry, I realized something powerful: Personal transformation is the foundation of sales success.

You cannot sell a vision of success to others if you are trapped in fear, doubt, or limiting beliefs. Sales is about trust. And trust begins with clarity, conviction, and confidence in what you offer.

To *Teach to Sell*, you must first become the product of the transformation you guide others through.

Personal development became my competitive edge—fueling my growth, shaping my goals, and ultimately leading to embracing the Self-Coaching Model.

It wasn't just about business. It was about becoming who I was meant to be.

PRE-DECISION COMPASS

Before applying *Teach to Sell*, ask yourself:

- What limiting belief is holding me back from achieving success?
- How have my past experiences shaped my perception of what's possible?
- What small, courageous step can I take today to move forward?
- How can I embrace uncertainty and trust that clarity comes through action?

By answering these questions, you ensure that you are stepping into the role of a leader, not just for yourself but for those you serve.

PRE-DECISION TO MAKE

You can **Pre-Decide** that when fear and doubt arise, you will recognize them not as stop signs but as markers that you're on the edge of growth. Instead of retreating, you will commit to taking action despite the discomfort, knowing that confidence is built through movement, not hesitation.

THE SELF-COACHING MODEL

The way we experience the world through our senses—what we see, hear, smell, taste, and touch—shapes our thoughts. Our thoughts influence our emotions, our emotions drive our actions, and our actions create our results. Simply put, success isn't just about what happens to us, it's about how we choose to respond.

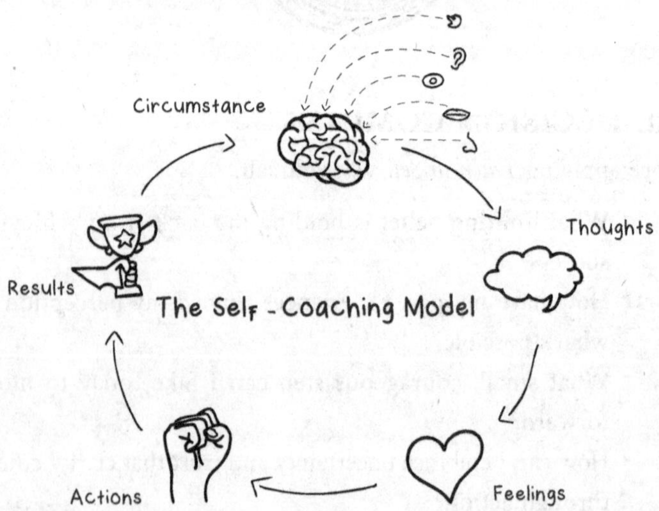

This cycle underscores a critical truth: **your habits determine your life**.

If you want to sell with confidence, build trust, and lead others to transformation, you must first **train yourself** to shift from reacting to life's circumstances to designing your outcomes with intention.

This is where daily practice makes the difference. By consistently aligning your mind, body, and emotions with success, you reinforce the very clarity and conviction that make you a powerful guide for others.

Here are the core practices that support this transformation:

1. **Prayer**—Align with your higher purpose.
2. **Meditation**—Quiet the mind and access deeper clarity.
3. **Affirmations**—Program yourself for success.
4. **Visualization**—Train your brain to achieve what it sees.
5. **Exercise**—Strengthen your body and sharpen your mind.
6. **Reading**—If you want to learn, read. But remember, if you want to truly master a subject, teach it!
7. **Gratitude**—Rewire your focus from lack to abundance.

Committing to at least one of these each day builds the foundation for transformation—within yourself and in the people you serve.

Transformation isn't just a personal journey; it's the secret weapon of every top performer in sales. The more intentional you are about **who you become**, the more effortlessly you will *Teach to Sell* and inspire others to take action.

PRAYER: ALIGNING WITH PURPOSE

Prayer is a direct line to your higher self, fostering peace, clarity, and resilience. It shifts focus from problems to solutions and deepens the connection to something greater than yourself.

How do you begin?

Set aside quiet time daily. Express gratitude, seek guidance, and affirm your purpose. Consistency strengthens this practice.

MEDITATE: REPROGRAMMING YOUR SUBCONSCIOUS

Meditation shifts brain waves from surface-level chaos to deep relaxation, unlocking the subconscious where true transformation happens.

The impact?

Reduced stress, improved clarity, and the ability to rewrite limiting beliefs. A calm mind creates space for remarkable growth.

How do you start?

1. **Find a quiet space**. Eliminate distractions and sit comfortably.
2. **Focus on your breath**. Breathe deeply and slowly.
3. **Clear your mind**. Let thoughts pass without attachment.
4. **Use guided meditation if needed**. Visit the *Transformational NLP Affirmations for Sales Success* Playlist on https://www.youtube.com/nobrokemonths.
5. **Commit to doing it five to ten minutes daily**. Increase gradually over time.

AFFIRM

Whether you realize it or not, you are affirming all the time. You might as well choose what you are telling yourself.

Does it matter what you tell yourself?

Some people claim a negative affirmation when they make a mistake. For example, they might say to themselves,

"I'm just clumsy."

or

"That was dumb."

Unfortunately, these negative statements often become a reality.

Positive statements about yourself also become a reality. You can program yourself by using positive declarations each morning. It would be best if you frequently exercised these positive statements to see the most favorable results.

HOW DO YOU GET THE BEST RESULTS FROM AFFIRMATIONS?

When you carry out affirmations regularly, they reinforce the connections between the neurons in your brain, allowing you to deliberately influence the message your mind hears, strengthening the relationship between the neurons.

> Affirm that your mind, body, and spirit are always calm.

To be most effective, affirmations should be:

1. Stated in the present tense
2. Share a positive statement
3. Believed by you
4. Short and specific
5. Honest

To supercharge your affirmations, consider writing them with pen and paper at least ten times daily. Writing stimulates your reticular activating system (RAS), which is the part of the brain that controls its consciousness. (Thomas, 2019)

HOW DO YOU BEGIN USING AFFIRM-ATIONS TO PROGRAM YOUR MIND?

You could select a broader affirmation that you dwell on for an extended period and add a few others each day.

I write a few affirmations each day to embrace other areas of my life that I intend to improve.

Some examples of affirmations that you could use include:

- I am a leader.
- I am a loving father/mother.
- I am worthy of reaching my goals.
- I step up.
- I believe in myself.
- I embrace the lead generation.
- I easily help ______ (fill in the blank) families buy my product or service each month.

VISUALIZE

How Does Visualization Work?

Visualization works because our brains interpret it as real life. When you form a mental image of what you intend to happen, you create a new pathway in the nervous system that strengthens your mind to act in a way that aligns with what you imagine.

> Consistently work to elevate your self-image

What Is a Real-Life Example of Visualization Working?

Many years ago, the visualization of living in the home of my dreams began.

The imagined house sat on at least five acres of rolling hills in horse country. It included an upscale swimming pool with a hot tub, a bathhouse with a gym, steam room, and sauna. Massive trees flanked the long driveway leading to the house, and the landscaped grounds had an attractive curb appeal.

Living in congested Northern Virginia, filled with people, traffic, and urban sprawl, made this seem like a tall order. Very few communities in the area offer large lots.

At that time, I lived in a cramped townhome in Alexandria, VA, and rented out the basement to Mark, a professional personal driver in his late fifties, before Airbnb and Uber were popular.

Still working at the restaurant, the pathway to the dream home was unclear, yet the destination was vivid. The visualization of living in that dream home persisted for years.

How Did This Visualization Become a Reality?

A few years later, I had the privilege of mentoring a promising real estate agent, Oscar Rodriguez. While guiding him in the business, we met a homeowner who had reached out for help selling their distressed property, a five-acre lot in Clifton, VA.

At the time, I was still finding my footing in real estate myself. I wasn't an expert, just someone willing to figure things out, take action, and help others along the way. If I could do this, truly, anyone could.

When we arrived, a scene of neglect and challenge greeted us. The once-maintained lawn had grown wild, swallowing the remnants of a driveway, which had since turned into a muddy path. We later learned that the owners had started renovations but ran out of money, leaving the driveway unfinished and the home in disrepair.

As we walked the property, I pointed out the concrete pad where a deck had once stood above. On one side, exposed cinder blocks held up eroded ground. On the other, the house loomed—its windows boarded up, a ghost of what it had once been.

Inside, the reality was even harsher. The overwhelming scent of dog urine and feces hit us instantly. The owners, elderly and struggling, had spent the past thirty years rescuing animals, but without the resources to maintain the home, it had fallen into ruin.

Ceilings sagged. Electrical fixtures barely functioned. Every step on the worn floors stirred up dust and memories of a home long past its prime.

I had no idea how we were going to sell this house.

But we had made a promise to the owners to help them move forward, to find a way when it seemed impossible. So, we took the listing, even though, at the time, I had no clue how we would fulfill that promise.

Driving back to the office, I turned to Oscar and admitted,

"I have no idea how we will sell that property."

Without hesitation, Oscar looked at me and said,

"You know, Dan, that is your dream home."

I laughed. It seemed ridiculous. But as his words settled, something shifted.

I began to see what he saw—not the wreck it was, but the potential it held.

The house was in terrible shape, but it sat on a beautiful hilltop, overlooking fifteen acres of the neighbor's clear rolling land. The surrounding homes were upscale.

The bones were there; it just needed someone to see beyond the mess.

So, I took a leap of faith.

It's been many years since I bought that home. Today, it's simply stunning.

If you visited today, you'd drive up to a beautifully crafted stone mailbox at the entrance. Red maple trees line the long driveway, guiding you to an elegant flagstone circular drive.

The house itself, once an eyesore, now stands as a testament to vision and persistence. Ledge stone veneer wraps around the columns supporting the gabled roof, and the exterior blends painted brick with classic Hardie-plank siding.

Inside, floor-to-ceiling windows frame breathtaking views from every room.

Step outside, and a spacious Trex deck stretches over a hundred feet, leading to a covered bridge I built to connect my mom's house to the main residence.

Beyond the bridge, strategically placed stone steps wind down to a custom-built pool—twenty feet wide and forty feet long, with an automatic cover. The travertine border adds elegance, and a tanning ledge with an umbrella slot offers the perfect space to unwind.

Lush landscaping surrounds the property, featuring black-eyed Susans, Winter Gem boxwood, and day lilies, adding warmth and color throughout the seasons.

This is more than just a house; it's the physical manifestation of a dream that I visualized long before I had any idea how it would come true. I am grateful for this home every day.

It reminds me that success isn't about having all the answers before you start. It's about taking the first step, trusting the process, and staying committed to the vision, even when it seems impossible.

If I, someone who once knew nothing about real estate, could turn a seemingly unsellable house into my dream home, then you can turn your own vision into reality.

Visualization works when you take action.

How Can You Use Visualization to Help You Make More Sales?

As a salesperson, I continue to leverage visualization, envisioning ten successful transactions monthly with ease. The results speak for themselves—exceeding client expectations, helping them achieve their dreams, and overcoming obstacles.

Visualization is not merely wishful thinking; it's a process that engages the subconscious mind. As thoughts manifest into actions, they guide our conscious mind and evoke emotions, shaping our reality in ways we may not have thought possible.

What Are the Direct Results of Visualization?

As we begin to visualize, our subconscious mind will take those thoughts and process them for us to act. We deliver this to our conscious mind through feedback we interpret as our thoughts. These thoughts also direct our emotions.

EXERCISE

Physical Exercise Helps the Entire Body, Including Your Brain

When you exercise, endorphins from your central nervous system are released. Endorphins help you be happier, less stressed, and experience greater levels of peace.

If you do not currently exercise, consider taking a walk each day. Even if you go for a short fifteen-minute walk, you will feel better and improve your mood. You could also join a gym with a friend or attend a fitness class.

READING

Harry S. Truman once said,

"Not all readers are leaders, but all leaders are readers."

Ask yourself,

"What would be different if I were to read ten pages of a book each morning instead of watching the news or checking my social media feed?"

High achievers read regularly. You learn and often get inspired to make great choices when you read. People have lived before us and have left clues about success and failure.

EXPRESSING GRATITUDE

Expressing gratitude transforms our mindset, enhances our happiness, and helps us focus on the positive aspects of life. By acknowledging what we are thankful for, we shift our attention from what we lack to the abundance we already possess.

How Does Expressing Gratitude Help Us?

Gratitude reduces stress, improves physical health, and strengthens relationships. It fosters a positive outlook, increases self-esteem, and enhances mental resilience. Regularly expressing gratitude creates a cycle of positivity that attracts us to be better in our lives.

How Do You Begin Using Gratitude to Enrich Your Life?

Start by keeping a gratitude journal. Each day, write down three things you are thankful for. They can be as simple as a sunny day, a kind gesture from a friend, or a personal achievement. Reflecting on these moments helps you cultivate a habit of gratitude, leading to a more joyful and fulfilling life.

What Could You Do to Use One or More of the Above?

Consider selecting one of the above meditation, affirmations, visualization, exercise, reading, or regularly expressing gratitude practices and carry out this activity each day for the next two months. After you master the first habit, try the following practice, master that pattern, create the following routine, and so on.

DISCIPLINE LEADS TO HABIT, WHICH LEADS TO SUCCESS

How Do You Remain Disciplined to Do the Steps to Reach the End of the Pathway That Will Allow You to Reach Your Goals?

Here is a secret I never shared. Successful people are not smart. Success is not a sign of intelligence; it results from implementing habits one small step at a time.

I currently sit in a Dunkin' Donuts as I write this. That is not a problem.

The challenge that I have experienced is that when I allow myself to visit the donut shop each day, I tend to get fat.

Luckily, I also enjoy the habit of working out each day. But unfortunately, due to my paradoxical relationship between exercise and pastries, I teeter between fitness and fatness.

When I embrace the discipline to say "no" to sweets, avoiding donuts, cakes, and pies becomes a habit. When I develop the practice consistently, I will have the success I desire.

Author, podcaster, entrepreneur, and retired Navy Seal Jocko Willink once stated,

Freedom is what everyone wants—to be able to act and live with freedom. But the only way to get to a place of freedom is through discipline.

If you want financial freedom, you must have financial discipline. If you want more free time, you must follow a more disciplined time management system.

You also must have the discipline to say "No" to things that eat up your time with no payback—things like random YouTube videos, click-bait on the internet, and even events that you agree to attend when you know you will not want to be there.

Discipline equals freedom applies to every aspect of life: if you want more freedom, get more discipline. (Willink, 2015)

The hardest part of any habit is in the beginning. I recommend you take small steps at a time.

TEACH TO SELL EXERCISE: OVERCOMING FEAR AND TAKING ACTION

1. Identify one area in your business or life where fear is holding you back.

____

____

____

2. Write down the worst possible outcome that your fear is telling you will happen.

____

____

____

3. Now write down the best possible outcome if you take action despite the fear.

____

____

____

4. Commit to one action today that moves you toward the best outcome.

____

____

____

5. Reflect at the end of the day: Did the worst-case scenario happen, or was the fear just an illusion?

____

____

____

CHAPTER SUMMARY: YOUR PATH TO SUCCESS

This chapter is about transformation—the shift from fear and doubt to clarity and action. Success in sales, business, and life isn't about having all the answers; it's about taking action before you feel ready.

Key Takeaways

- **You don't need perfect conditions to start**—just a commitment to growth.
- *Teach to Sell* **is about embodying transformation** so that you can guide others through it.
- **Visualization plus action and self-belief turn the impossible into reality.**
- **Your daily habits define your success;** small, consistent actions lead to breakthroughs.

Success isn't about talent, it's about committing to the journey, knowing that both setbacks and victories are part of the process. By following the path outlined in this chapter, you'll gain a clearer roadmap to success and learn to embrace the journey—challenges and all—with greater confidence and fulfillment.

Commit or Quit Challenge: Will You Do the Work?

Every hero reaches a crossroads—a moment when they must choose between staying in their comfort zone or stepping into the unknown to claim a better future.

That moment is now.

Will you stay trapped by the beliefs and habits that have held you back, or will you take the first step toward transforming your future?

Here's your challenge:

1. Identify one fear or limiting belief that has kept you from reaching your full potential in sales or life.
2. Take one action today—no matter how small—that directly challenges that belief
3. Share this commitment with a mentor, friend, or accountability partner.
4. Track your progress for one week and reflect on how this small shift creates momentum.

The greatest salespeople, entrepreneurs, and leaders weren't born fearless—they learned to take action despite fear. If you truly want change, commit. If not, quit before wasting another day stuck in fear.

Will you Commit or Quit?

CHAPTER 5

Upgrade Your Environment

A DEFINING MOMENT IN MY REAL ESTATE JOURNEY

I had been a real estate agent for eighteen months, working tirelessly in a struggling brokerage. Every day, I faced the grind, determined to carve out my success.

One morning, two top agents from another branch of our franchise approached me with a proposition. They were buying our brokerage and wanted my support.

By then, I was the top-selling agent, and they knew having me on their team would be a game-changer. I agreed to the discussion and asked about opportunities for myself.

After much negotiation, we settled on my becoming a partner with a 20 percent stake. Then, they offered me the role of controlling partner.

At first, I hesitated. A part of me feared my new partners were using me as a frontman. I believed the regional owners didn't like them and wouldn't approve their ownership.

At the time, they each owned more shares of the organization than I did, and I knew I needed complete control to make a difference.

Quickly, I realized these partners weren't the right fit for me, but I had already signed the agreements and committed.

That's when Rene Giesberts, a kind colleague from the Netherlands who played drums in a band, invited me to lunch. He asked,

"Dan, you're investing a lot here. Do you trust either of the ladies to lead?"

His words hit me hard. I paused and reflected. The answer was clear—I didn't.

That was the moment I chose to rise above my doubts and fully embrace my potential. I took the role, stepped into the challenge, and committed to transforming the brokerage.

Rene, who later tragically passed away from brain cancer, had given me the clarity I needed. His insight changed everything for me.

I stepped into leadership, ready to transform my environment and fulfill my potential. That moment marked the beginning of my belief in myself.

PRE-DECISION COMPASS: SHAPING YOUR SUCCESS THROUGH ENVIRONMENT

Reflect on the key moments where your environment has either propelled you forward or held you back. Assessing your surroundings is the first step in upgrading your environment.

Ask yourself:

- Who are the people I spend the most time with? Do they inspire or drain me?
- What limiting beliefs about my environment have I accepted as truth?
- What small changes can I make today to create a more empowering space for growth?
- If I fully believed in my potential, what would I do differently?

PRE-DECISION TO MAKE

You can **Pre-Decide** that when faced with an opportunity that could elevate your environment, you will choose to embrace it rather than hesitate in fear. You will recognize the power of your surroundings and proactively shape them to support your growth.

THE POWER OF BELIEF

Believing in yourself might be a challenge for some. However, there are steps you can take to increase your self-belief.

When coaching executives today, I examine their entire life context, not just their business environment.

If you want to sell effectively, you must shift your perspective from internal self-doubt to external understanding. The more you align with how others think and feel, the greater your influence.

Whether you're an executive, an entrepreneur, or someone striving for personal and professional growth, these strategies will help you enhance your decision-making, build confidence, and cultivate resilience.

Here are ten ways to believe in yourself.

1) CHANGE YOUR PERSPECTIVE

Success in sales (or any endeavor) comes with setbacks. The bigger your goals, the greater the potential for failure.

But failure is not a dead end; it's a lesson. Instead of seeing rejection as a defeat, view it as feedback that guides you toward growth.

Do the following simple exercise and permanently transform your approach to failure and rejection.

Teach to Sell Exercise:

Think of a time you failed in your sales career and write it down.

____

____

____

____

Rewrite that experience as a learning opportunity. What did you gain from it?

____

____

____

____

Learn from your missteps, bounce back, and persist toward achieving your goals.

2) TRANSFORM YOUR LIMITING BELIEFS

Negative emotions—self-doubt, fear, and anxiety—are rooted in how you interpret past experiences. Reframing your thoughts changes everything.

Teach to Sell Exercise:

Recall a time when you felt unworthy or full of doubt. Write that down.

____

____

____

____

Identify the beliefs that fueled those feelings.

____

____

____

____

Rewrite those beliefs into empowering statements.
For example, in the answers above, you might have said something like,

> "I'm not good at sales because I hate being pushy."

You could rewrite this as,

"Sales is about serving, not pushing. I help people make the best decisions for their needs. The more I listen and provide value, the more successful I become."

____

____

____

____

A way to defeat your limiting beliefs is to be more aware of the words you use when talking to yourself.

So, the next time you realize that you are talking to yourself negatively, replace those negative thoughts with positive statements.

3) LOVE YOURSELF

Self-confidence begins with self-awareness and self-love. Acknowledge your strengths and appreciate yourself.

Teach to Sell Exercise:

List three traits you love about yourself.

____

____

____

____

Mastering the art of self-awareness and self-love is the first step in getting the art of self-confidence.

4) EMBRACE HEALTHY ROUTINES

Your subconscious mind dictates your outcomes more than your conscious thoughts. The pathway from the subconscious to the conscious allows your thoughts to manifest results. The more you establish positive habits, the more control you gain over your success.

Teach to Sell Exercise:

Identify a habit you need to adopt to support your growth.

____

____

____

____

Who will hold you accountable for implementing this new habit?

____

____

____

____

Commit to practicing it daily for the next thirty days.

5) SURROUND YOURSELF WITH SUPPORTIVE PEOPLE

Your environment influences your success. Surround yourself with people who elevate you and support your growth.

Teach to Sell Exercise:

Identify one person who uplifts you.

Commit to spending an extra hour with that person this week.

6) CREATE A "BOARD OF DIRECTORS" IN YOUR MIND

A "Board of Directors" exists in my mind, providing counsel when advice is needed.

For example, when facing a losing battle in sales, business, or personal life, consulting the ancient Chinese general Sun Tzu, author of *The Art of War*, reveals the wisdom to pass on a fight that cannot be won and live for another day.

A few of my "Board of Directors" include:

- Tony Robbins
- Eckhart Tolle
- Dale Carnegie
- Jack Welch
- Arnold Schwarzenegger
- and others

Additionally, lesser-known individuals, who may not be recognized, are also part of this advisory group.

Teach to Sell Exercise:

Choose a successful individual you admire.

(It could be Walt Disney, Benjamin Franklin, myself, or anyone else with a perceived success you would like to know about.)

____

____

Commit to reading or listening to their biography. Seek their guidance in your mind when facing challenges.

What would Walt Disney say about creativity? What timeless wisdom would Benjamin Franklin drop on discipline and opportunity? What advice would I give you about sales?

7) STOP COMPARING

Have you ever been jealous of another or not like someone (even if you never met them) for no good reason? If so, you are comparing your insides with their outside.

Instead of comparing yourself to others, express gratitude and focus on what you have. By focusing on what you have and expressing gratitude, you move from a scarcity mindset to one of abundance.

Concentrating on what you are grateful for will shift your mindset from scarcity to abundance.

Teach to Sell Exercise:

Identify a person you've judged.

____

____

____

Find a trait about them you can appreciate.

____

____

____

____

List three things you're grateful for today.

____

____

____

____

8) FACE YOUR FEARS

What scares you?

What will hold you back?

Do not worry. Fears are standard; the good news is you can embrace fear and TAKE ACTION anyway.

I assure you that you CAN succeed.

Take a moment to consider your existence. You are a spiritual being in a physical manifestation of 37.2 trillion (said another way, 37,200,000 million) cells! (Milo & Phillips, 2015)

When you understand that our reality expands beyond our comprehension, it becomes easier to approach the things that scare you.

You are a spiritual being in a physical manifestation. Your mind is infinite, and you can assign meaning to anything.

You can create lead generation to be a thing to fear, or you can create lead generation as something to embrace. The choice is yours.

Teach to Sell Exercise:

Identify something in sales that scares you.

____

____

____

Assign a new, empowering meaning to that fear.

____

____

____

9) LEARN A NEW SKILL

Acquiring new knowledge not only promotes the formation of neural connections but also enhances your decision-making abilities.

Furthermore, mastering a new skill instills confidence in oneself and strengthens belief in one's abilities.

Teach to Sell Exercise:

Identify a skill you want to learn.

____

____

____

____

Commit to taking one action today toward mastering it.

10) ACT TODAY

Procrastination is the enemy of progress. The key to success? Taking action NOW.

Teach to Sell Exercise:

What's one thing you've been putting off?

____

____

____

When will you do it?

____

____

____

CHAPTER SUMMARY: UPGRADE YOUR ENVIRONMENT

Your environment is either pushing you forward or holding you back. This chapter explores how to take control of your surroundings to foster growth and success.

Key Takeaways

- **Your success is deeply influenced by the people and surroundings** you choose.
- **Changing your perspective on failure transforms obstacles** into stepping stones.
- **Surrounding yourself with the right people** accelerates your growth.
- **Face fears and take decisive** action builds confidence.
- **Success is a choice**; commit to upgrading your environment or remain stuck in mediocrity.

Commit or Quit Challenge: Will You Do the Work?

At some point, you must decide whether you will stay where you are or push forward into new opportunities. Change requires action, and action requires commitment.

- **Commit** to applying at least one of these strategies this week.
- **Quit** making excuses for why you can't start.

Your next level is waiting.

Will you Commit or Quit?

CHAPTER 6

Teach to Create and Achieve Your Goals

A FATHER'S LESSON IN UNCERTAINTY

I was thirty-eight years old, and my wife at the time, Traci, and I wanted to have a baby. After our devastating fourth miscarriage, we decided to adopt.

We hired an adoption agency in Ohio while living in Virginia. Background checks, home studies, and interviews became our routine, each step bringing us closer to welcoming a child into our family.

Then, one morning, we received a call. A teenage girl in Tennessee was preparing to give birth, and we had been chosen. But just a week before the delivery, the girl's aunt decided to raise the child instead.

The emotional rollercoaster was brutal. We had bonded with a child we would never meet.

A few weeks later, after returning from a fishing trip in Alaska with my dad, my phone rang again.

"There's a baby being born in Las Vegas in two days. Do you want to be considered?"

Three hours later, we were on a plane.

COMMITMENT IN THE FACE OF UNCERTAINTY

I wasn't afraid to become a father; I was afraid to love again, only to lose. Four times before, I had loved an unborn child, and four times, my heart shattered, unable to hold those precious lives in my arms.

By the time we arrived in Las Vegas, the situation had already turned into a negotiation. The birth parents wanted us to buy them a trailer. I wasn't willing to barter for my baby, so I left it in the hands of attorneys and God.

The next day, I was in the hospital cafeteria, unsure what would happen.

The social worker called me, saying,

"Come sign some paperwork."

And just like that, my life changed.

Holding Maggie for the first time in my hands—well, *hand*, because she was so tiny—was the most defining moment of my life.

All the heartbreaks before that moment were worth it. I was a father to a beautiful girl we named Maggie, and instantly fell in love.

We had to stay in Nevada for a few weeks until the court approved the adoption. Traci returned to Virginia, and I remained alone with Maggie while we waited.

On the fourteenth floor of the ARIA Hotel, I made her a promise:

"You can own this entire building, or you can sleep homeless at its doorstep. Either way, I'll love you. But I hope you choose greatness, health, and success."

As a dad, I realized I was already teaching her about life and love.

That was the first time I *taught* my daughter anything—how to make choices.

PRE-DECISION COMPASS: THE POWER OF TEACHING AND TRANSFORMATION

Before you take action on any goal, ask yourself:

- What experiences shaped your current beliefs?
- Where have you held yourself back due to fear or uncertainty?
- What false narratives have stopped you from achieving more?
- What would happen if you fully committed to your goals and trusted the process?

PRE-DECISION TO MAKE

From now on, you will embrace teaching as a path to mastery.

- When challenges arise, you will look for the lesson, not the excuse.
- You will lead with clarity, making decisions that align with your true goals.

- You will use the *Teach to Sell* method to build trust, guide others, and position yourself as an authority.

Teaching is not just about helping others—it's about reinforcing your own learning and growth.

TEACH TO SELL: WHY TEACHING IS THE ULTIMATE PATH TO MASTERY

Later, my mantra grew to share with Maggie and others: to have the best day of your life, make good choices, help someone, and always, always be grateful.

My world was unfamiliar, yet I was committed to the journey.

Looking back, I realize I was already practicing *Teach to Sell*. Teaching isn't just about providing information; it's about helping others navigate life's uncertainties and make empowered decisions.

Teaching transforms you. It forces clarity, builds trust, and positions you as an authority. It's the reason I became a better father, business owner, and sales professional.

HOW DOES TEACHING HELP YOU BECOME AN EXPERT?

In my early years as a real estate brokerage owner, I needed to boost my confidence in understanding the technical details of contracts, legal issues, risk management, and other crucial aspects.

To deepen my knowledge, I started teaching a principles class to help individuals obtain their real estate licenses.

Recognizing that teaching would enhance my understanding, I chose this approach as the most effective way to master the material.

Teaching hundreds of agents to obtain their licenses has provided an additional advantage: it has contributed to my success as an agent.

The trust cultivated among the agents I've taught translates into increased trust and benefit for my clients, as these agents are eager to collaborate with me.

WHY DOES TEACHING TRANSFORM YOU?

Teaching is one of the most powerful ways to build trust and establish yourself as an authority. When you teach, you share your knowledge openly, demonstrating your expertise and willingness to help others. This builds credibility and rapport, making clients more likely to trust and follow your guidance.

LEAD: THE *TEACH TO SELL* FRAMEWORK FOR MASTERY

The LEAD acronym stands for **Learn, Embrace, Acquire, Demonstrate**. It defines how *Teach to Sell* helps you master your craft and lead others:

- **Learn** established frameworks and models.
- **Embrace** a proven system for success.
- **Acquire** deep knowledge in your field.
- **Demonstrate** expertise by teaching others.

THE POWER OF TEACHING: HOW I BECAME AN AUTHORITY IN REAL ESTATE

In my early years as a real estate broker, I lacked confidence in the technical side of the business—contracts, legalities, risk management.

To deepen my expertise, I decided to teach.

I started instructing real estate principles classes. The more I taught, the more I mastered the material. Soon, hundreds of agents I had trained saw me as a trusted expert, making negotiations and collaborations easier.

The same applies to *any* industry. Teaching builds trust, and trust drives influence.

TEACH TO SELL IN SALES: ADDRESSING CLIENT FEARS BEFORE THEY SURFACE

Imagine you're a real estate agent working with a homebuyer. The moment they make an offer, they'll experience:

- Anxiety over whether they made the right decision
- Fear of financial uncertainty
- Doubt triggered by friends or family

Now, imagine two different sales experiences:

1. An **average agent** who never mentions this rollercoaster of emotions.

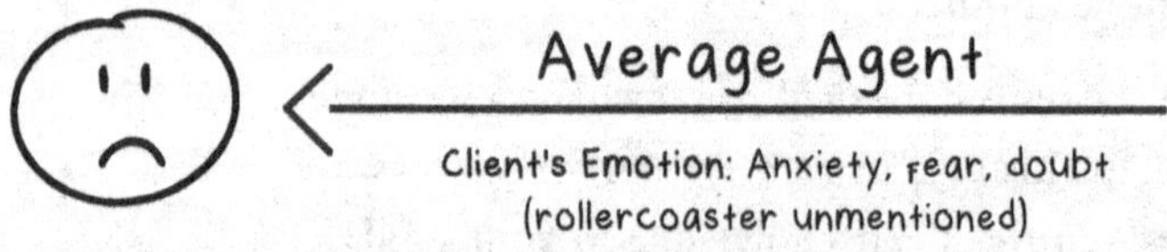

2. A *Teach to Sell* **agent** who explains the entire process before it happens, preparing the client in advance.

Which agent builds trust? Which client feels more secure?

Addressing emotions before they arise is one of the most powerful ways to gain influence.

No matter what your sales profession, consider your client's emotional journey. Address it upfront to instill confidence in their future decisions. Addressing these concerns before they arise will ease your clients' anxieties and build stronger, more trusting relationships.

By teaching, you transform your skills into a powerful force. You gain mastery over your abilities and create an environment of trust and respect. Your clients see you as a dependable guide, ensuring your success is not just possible but inevitable.

TEACH TO SELL EXERCISE: TAKING CHARGE OF YOUR LIFE

What doubts and feelings of unworthiness have held you back?

____

____

____

____

Who can guide you toward success?

____

____

____

____

What specific steps can you take today toward your dreams?

____

____

____

____

How can you embrace gratitude and create your best day?

____

____

____

By applying these exercises, you're not just learning, you're building a future where you lead others through transformation.

FINAL THOUGHTS: TEACHING IS THE KEY TO EVERYTHING

When I look back on my journey—from the heartbreak of miscarriages and failed adoptions to the moment I held Maggie in my hands—I see a single truth:

> Success isn't about luck. It's about _teaching_ yourself to think differently, to commit, to lead.

You cannot sell a vision of success if you're trapped in doubt. You cannot guide others until you learn to guide yourself.

You cannot _Teach to Sell_ until you master the transformation you want others to experience.

The secret to sales success? **Become the teacher of your craft.**

CHAPTER SUMMARY: TEACHING CREATES MASTERY AND SUCCESS

- **Teaching is the best way to learn.** When you teach, you reinforce knowledge and build trust.
- **The LEAD framework creates experts.** Learn, Embrace, Acquire, Demonstrate.
- **Addressing client fears builds trust**. Explaining the journey in advance eliminates uncertainty.
- *Teach to Sell* **is about empowerment.** The more you teach, the more clarity and confidence you create—for yourself and others.

Commit or Quit Challenge: Break the Cycle or Stay Stuck

You can continue...

- Struggling to define your goals
- Letting fear control your decisions
- Wasting time with trial and error

Or you can commit to...

- Learning a proven framework
- Teaching others to gain mastery
- Building trust through clarity and leadership

Success isn't about talent. It's about focus, commitment, and the ability to teach others to see a new path forward.

Will you Commit or Quit?

CHAPTER 7

Teach to Transform

THE CHOICES THAT DEFINE US

I was five years clean and sober, and my world felt vibrant again. My business was growing, my confidence was strong, and I was proving to myself that transformation was possible.

A huge part of that success was Dave, the man who had been my anchor through early recovery. He was my trusted business partner managing our house-flipping projects. He was the kind of guy you'd want in your corner. Dependable. Strong. But something was off. I hadn't heard from him in days.

On my way to the airport for a conference in Florida, I took a detour to check on one of our renovation projects. The site was at a standstill. No workers. No progress. Something wasn't right.

From Florida, I called Dave again. No answer.

I reached out to his wife, Rebecca. Her voice, choked with emotion, shattered the silence:

"Dave is in the hospital."

I rushed home. The moment I walked into his hospital room, I knew this wasn't just a setback. A nurse adjusted the tube running through his collarbone, and the doctor's words were blunt—his liver was failing. One more drink, and he would die.

Four days later, he was discharged.

A week later, he had a beer.

The descent was swift, brutal, unstoppable.

I took Maggie, my toddler, to visit Dave in home hospice. Some might question why I brought her, but I saw an opportunity—an opportunity to *Teach to Sell*. Not in the way you might think. This wasn't about business. It was about something bigger: helping her understand life, choice, and consequence.

Dave, once thriving, was now a shadow. Yet, in his final days, he smiled—peaceful, knowing, accepting.

I knelt beside Maggie and told her:

"Life isn't about right or wrong. It's about outcomes. Every choice leads somewhere."

Dave wasn't a bad person. He wasn't wrong. But his choices had led him here, dying before forty-five.

Three weeks later, hospice called. Dave was being moved for his final hours.

I was too weak to drive. My friend Danny took me. I kissed Dave on the forehead.

Two hours later, Dave died.

LESSONS FROM TRAGEDY

Dave's story is heartbreaking, but it holds a powerful lesson.
Life is shaped by our choices. Some push us forward, while others keep us stuck in painful cycles.

Teach to Sell is built on this very idea: **people don't change because they're told to. They change because they're led to see a better way.**

Had Dave been able to shift his perspective, to see the power of his choices differently, his story might have ended differently. But without the right guidance—without someone leading him to *sell himself* on a better future—he remained trapped in a pattern he couldn't break.

The truth is, most people don't realize how much their past controls them. But there's a way to break free.

And that's where a powerful tool comes in.

So, what is this tool that can rewrite our future?

It's called neuro-linguistic programming (NLP).

NLP is a way to understand how our thoughts and words shape our actions and results. It's the foundation of *Teach to Sell*; when you understand how people think, you can guide them to better decisions.

Sales, influence, leadership—it all comes down to the ability to shift someone's mindset. That begins with how we communicate.

By learning to shift our mindset and language, NLP helps us:

- Avoid big mistakes, both in business and life.
- Break destructive patterns before they become permanent.
- Create a better future with more success and confidence.

Had Dave understood this, his story could have been different.

Had I not learned this, my business would have failed.

Had I not applied this, I wouldn't have been able to *Teach to Sell*—whether in my personal life, remaining sober, helping my daughter understand choices, or in business, guiding clients toward the best decision.

This is why *Teach to Sell* isn't just about closing deals. It's about opening minds.

PRE-DECISION COMPASS: REWRITING THE NARRATIVE BEFORE IT'S TOO LATE

Before tragedy strikes, before a cycle repeats itself, before another poor decision is made, ask yourself:

- What patterns from my past are shaping my present choices?
- Am I reacting to circumstances or actively designing my life?
- What beliefs do I hold that could be limiting my potential?
- How can I reframe my challenges into opportunities for growth?

By answering these questions, you create awareness of the invisible forces driving your actions. This is the first step to transforming your future.

PRE-DECISION TO MAKE

You can **Pre-Decide** that every setback will be a learning opportunity.

Instead of letting the past dictate your future, you will commit to identifying your patterns, reshaping your perspective, and making conscious choices that serve your highest potential.

By doing this, you take control of your life instead of being controlled by it.

WHAT IS NLP AND WHY DOES IT MATTER IN *TEACH TO SELL?*

NLP, founded by John Grinder and Richard Bandler explores excellence and subjective experience, shaping our beliefs about ourselves and others.

NLP offers a framework for understanding and interpreting the world, empowering individuals to make conscious, empowered choices—choices I wish Dave had made.

By harnessing the power of NLP, you can navigate life's complexities with greater insight and effectiveness, shaping our destinies with purpose and intention.

HOW TEACH TO SELL USES NLP TO INFLUENCE AND LEAD

At its core, *Teach to Sell* is about understanding how people process the world:

- What they see
- What they feel
- What they hear
- The words they use

We often don't realize how our words dictate our experiences. By mastering **NLP's Three Principles**, we gain control over our outcomes:

- **Mind**—The limitless power we possess
- **Consciousness**—How we create our experiences
- **Thought**—Our awareness of our Mind and Consciousness

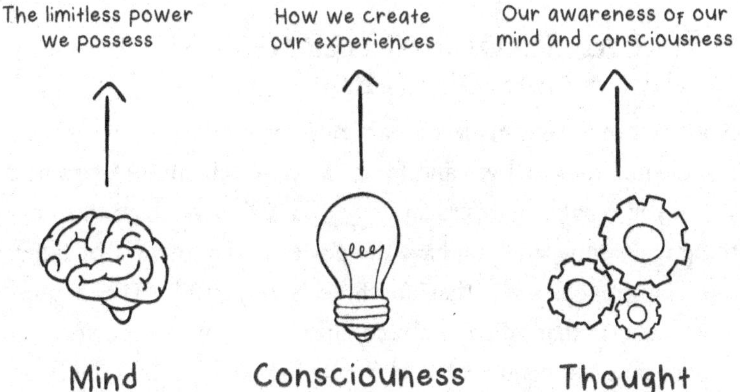

Want to be a better salesperson? A stronger leader? A happier human?

Master NLP. Master *Teach to Sell*.

Because when you understand how people make decisions, you can guide them toward success, whether in business, personal growth, or even in moments that truly matter.

Sometimes, that understanding can save a life.

I couldn't save Dave's life. That pain stays with me. But if these words reach just one person—if this book saves even one life—then every moment of this journey was worth it.

HOW DOES NLP HELP YOU IN SALES?

NLP is the combination of understandings, encounters, expectations, and ideas particular to a person. When you recognize your ability to think in this manner, you will learn how to use it to live a better life and become a better salesperson.

You can better lead, persuade, or motivate when you know what impacts you as much as a prospective or current client.

HOW CAN KNOWING NLP HELP US IN OTHER AREAS OF LIFE?

Nobody can "make" us feel a particular way. We are 100 percent responsible for our lives and for how we proclaim our existence. When you recognize this as a reality, you will understand that anything is possible, and you have the power to design your own life.

The great news is that anything is achievable. The not-so-great news is that when you recognize your limitless power, you never again can blame external events for your circumstances.

Former professional football quarterback Tom Brady summed up the sentiment regarding personal responsibility,

> "Too often in life, something happens, and we blame other people for us not being happy or satisfied or fulfilled.

> "So, the point is, we all have choices, and we choose to accept people or situations or not to accept situations." (Chiarella, 2008)

Brady did not always take personal responsibility for his actions. As a young man, he would blame others, such as his coach, teammates, the weather, and anything else, for justifying any struggles.

As Brady matured as a football player, he began to take full responsibility for his actions and results. He became "Tom Brady."

IF YES, THEN HOW?

Often, people have fantastic excuses to rationalize the obstacles that get in their way. You might have exceptional reasons.

I respect your rationale, and I encourage you to take a step back and ask,

"Is there another way? How can this be done?"

Sometimes life presents us with scenarios that give us one choice. When this happens, challenge the situation.

Ask yourself,

"Is it possible to be a world-class mom AND a highly successful salesperson?"

and if your answer is,

"Yes,"

then ask,

"How?"

Moreover, if you cannot see the way to "How?" ask the most crucial question,

"Why?"

Maybe you are making sales to pay your bills. Perhaps you are in sales to pay for your kid to go to private school or build a home for your mother (Yes, this is possible as not long ago, I finished a two-year project to build my mother's house.

Yes, I said,

"TWO YEARS!"

While my choice of contractors was wrong, I am responsible for having selected the vendor.)

DELETION, DISTORTION, AND GENERALIZATION

The language you unintentionally use could generate uncertainty, confusion, and other difficulties that hinder your clients from pursuing their goals. When we speak with another person or ourselves, we often filter through

- Deletion
- Distortion
- Generalization

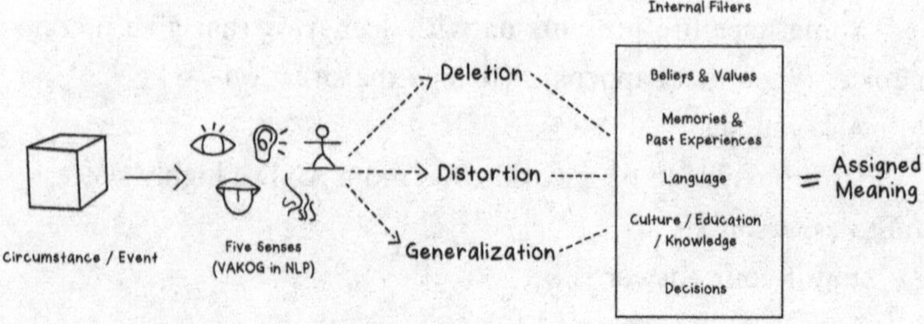

We screen the words and sounds we hear, the pictures we see, our feelings, self-talk, tastes, and smells through these omissions.

Deletion is when we perceive a part of what someone says as not relevant.

Distortion occurs when our bias pressures us to believe something we do not intend to consider.

Generalization is when we associate an occasion as representative of all future experiences. (Tripp, 2015)

Deletions, Distortions, and Generalizations can work for you when used strategically and can hurt your communication if you do not pay attention.

DELETION

What Do You Mean by Deletion in Communication?

Deletion happens when part of a message is left out, making it vague or open to interpretation.

For example:

> "People know they want a professional like me
> to help them."

But who are the "people"? What do they "know"? What kind of help do they want?

When we leave out details, we allow others to fill in the blanks with their own assumptions—sometimes to our advantage, sometimes leading to miscommunication.

The environment offers eleven million bits per second for our subconscious to process, yet we can be consciously aware of fewer than fifty bits of information per second. (Morin, 2015) We filter many millions of bits of information in a short period.

The fact that we can perceive a minuscule amount of info offered at any given moment means we can always find evidence to support our point of view.

Two or more people can have the same experience or be a part of the same environment and perceive knowledge to validate opposite opinions or experiences.

Is It Healthy to Compare Your Results to Other People's?

Success is subjective and personal. Therefore, our perception of others does not serve us except in studying the models of how other people achieve.

Do not judge your self-worth based on another person's social media highlight reel. Instead, define success based on your compass in the areas of life that are important to you and then determine success from those metrics.

Take a moment to consider how you define success.

- What is success?
- What does success look like to you?
- Is success about winning or money?

From 1948 to 1975, John Wooden coached the UCLA basketball team. During that time, his program won a fantastic ten national championships. His team's record was 664 wins–162 losses during his time as the coach. (ESPN, n.d.)

If you are a sports fan, you undoubtedly would agree that Coach Wooden is one of the most successful coaches ever.

But what did Wooden believe about success?

He said,

> "True success is attained only through the
> satisfaction of knowing you did everything
> within the limits of your ability to become
> the very best that you are capable of being."
> (Wooden & Jamison, 1997)

I understand Wooden's words to mean that when you focus on achieving your highest potential by doing something that brings you joy, the wins will follow.

What Should You Do If You Perceive Failure?

In some cases, I have failed in my efforts. But, of course, failure is as subjective as success. So, in no situation do I allow failure to define me. And neither should YOU!

Years ago, I had the honor of meeting Zig Ziglar at an event in Washington, DC. So, when I think of failure, I agree with Ziglar when he said,

> "A failure is an event, not a person."

How Can Deletion Harm Our Self-Talk?

We often delete important words in our thoughts, making our self-talk unclear and sometimes negative.

For example:

> "It can be hard to be successful in business."

But what exactly makes it hard? What does "success" even mean? Asking questions will allow you to gain clarity.

Or worse:

> "I'm not the kind of person who can succeed."

This vague, negative statement can reinforce limiting beliefs. Instead, ask yourself:

- "What makes me believe that?"
- "How can I succeed?"

By questioning vague statements, you gain clarity and reframe your mindset.

How Does Deletion Affect Communication with Others?

When we use words like:

> "Can't, not able, must, everybody, nobody,"

we create gaps in meaning, making it easy for misunderstandings to happen.

For example:

> "This is much better."

Better than what? How much better? Without context, the listener fills in the meaning themselves, which may not match what you intended.

Can Deletion Be Useful?

Yes. Skilled communicators use strategic deletion to guide thinking. For example:

- "Our team works harder."
- "This is the best solution."

These statements are persuasive because the listener defines "harder" or "best" in a way that resonates with them.

Takeaway

Deletion can cause confusion, but when used intentionally, it can make communication clearer, more persuasive, and more powerful.

DISTORTION

Distortion is when you understand communication to mean something you did not intend to convey.

When you make a statement in which one thing causes another, or your conjecture suggests mind-reading, or when one purposefully assigns meaning stated in the second part of a sentence on purpose from the first part, then you are demonstrating Distortion.

Example of Distortion

I once taught a seminar on how we process information—specifically, how we delete, distort, and generalize things we hear and see.

After class, a student asked me to explain Distortion further. I used an example from another lesson we covered: the Three Phases of Human Development.

- **Imprinting (ages 1–7):** Kids absorb beliefs that shape their future. This is like their programming stage.
- **Modeling (ages 8–12):** They start copying behaviors from those around them. If you don't want your child to text and drive later, don't check your phone at stoplights now!
- **Socialization (ages 12–21 for girls, 12–25 for boys):** Friends become more influential than family.

To illustrate, I mentioned my daughter, Maggie, who was eight at the time. I said,

"Maggie is now Modeling."

I meant she was at the stage where she learns by watching others. But the student misunderstood, thinking she was literally walking down a fashion runway!

That mix-up? A perfect example of Distortion—where someone interprets information in a way that changes its original meaning.

GENERALIZATION

Some of President Donald Trump's favorite phrases include:

"Everybody thinks this."

"Our party always does that."

"Many people are saying this."

He once tweeted,

"Many people are saying that the Iranians killed the scientist who helped the US because of Hillary Clinton's hacked emails." (Trump, 2016)

Trump is an expert at using Generalization in his communication.

However, to avoid alienating half of my readers by mentioning Trump's name, I would like to emphasize that presidents Bill Clinton, Barack Obama, and almost any other successful politician (yep, even George W. Bush) are all experts in persuasion. How else can you inspire half of the country to support you?

The most successful politicians are highly skilled in their ability to persuade others. Politicians and other influential people often use Generalization to achieve consensus, such as when they say,

> "Everybody agrees that we should implement this program."

What Are Generalizations?

Generalizations are comments that you may want to challenge by asking,

> "Who says?"

Or,

> "What evidence do you have for that statement?"

The essential words to pay attention to are:

- All
- Never
- Always
- Very

The above words simplify our worldview and restrain us in our interpretation.

For example:

- I never will be able to achieve my sales goals.
- No one cares if I succeed.
- I cannot see myself as a top producer.

How Can You Challenge a Generalization?

To challenge these Generalizations, ask for counterexamples, such as:

- Will you NEVER be able reach your goals? Has another person done so before you?
- Is there ANYONE who cares about your success?
- What is stopping you?

HOW TO USE NLP TO GUIDE AND PERSUADE

NLP is a powerful tool for sales, rooted in psychology and persuasion techniques. Here are some ways to use it in language:

1. **Tie-downs**—Encouraging agreement

Tie-downs are questions added to the end of a statement to subtly guide someone toward agreement.

These phrases work because they make it easy to say "Yes," reinforcing the idea in the listener's mind. Instead of making a direct claim, a tie-down invites them to confirm it themselves, reducing resistance.

Examples:

- "This will make your life easier, **won't it?**"
- "You want the best for your family, **don't you?**"
- "It makes sense to move forward now, **doesn't it?**"

By using tie-downs, you lead people to agree naturally, making them feel like they arrived at the decision on their own.

2. **Embedded commands**—Embedded commands are phrases that subtly guide someone's thinking without them realizing it.

The brain picks up on keywords (in capital letters) said with emphasis as a command (like you would tell your dog, "SIT!") and interprets them as instructions. This technique is often used in sales and persuasion to make decisions feel natural rather than forced.

Here's how it works:

- "As you **CONSIDER THIS**, you'll realize it's the right choice."
- "When you decide to **MOVE FORWARD**, you'll see the benefits."
- "You can **START NOTICING** how this fits perfectly into your plans."

3. **Future pacing**—Helping clients visualize success

Future pacing encourages people to picture themselves experiencing the benefits of a decision. By prompting them to imagine a positive future, it makes the outcome feel real and achievable.

This technique is powerful in sales and persuasion because once someone mentally steps into that future, they are more likely to act.

Examples:

- "Imagine six months from now, fully settled into using our new product or service."
- "Think about how relieved you'll feel once this is handled."
- "Picture yourself enjoying the results of this decision every day."

By painting a vivid picture of success, future pacing helps guide people toward making confident choices.

4. **Reframing**—Shifting perspective for a positive outlook

Reframing helps people see a situation differently, often turning obstacles into opportunities. Instead of focusing on perceived downsides, it shifts attention to the benefits, making a decision feel more appealing.

Examples:

- "This isn't just an expense; it's an investment in your future."
- "What if this decision is the key to unlocking your success?"
- "Instead of seeing this as a challenge, consider it an opportunity for growth."

By changing the way something is viewed, reframing reduces hesitation and encourages action.

Use these techniques to help, not to manipulate. They're meant to guide people toward confident, informed decisions.

Now that you know their power, you have a responsibility to use them ethically—to build trust, not pressure people. How you use them will shape your impact.

FINAL LESSON: *TEACH TO SELL* IS THE MOST POWERFUL INFLUENCE TOOL YOU HAVE

Had I understood the concepts of NLP and seeking excellence in life when I was younger, I would have seen how much influence I truly had.

Had my friend, Dave, understood it, he might still be here.

The ability to *Teach to Sell* is the ability to change lives. Because when you teach someone how to think differently, you empower them to make better choices.

And that is the ultimate transformation.

CHAPTER SUMMARY: *TEACH TO SELL*—THE POWER OF CHOICES IN TRANSFORMATION

Life is built on choices. Every decision either moves us forward or holds us back. I learned this the hard way through Dave—a brother to me, a trusted business partner—whose choices led him to an early death.

His story isn't about good or bad, it's about actions and outcomes. Every choice has consequences, and yours shape your future.

Whether in business, sales, or life, success comes down to how you think, communicate, and influence. *Teach to Sell* ensures you're always leading with value—educating, guiding, and empowering others to make the best decisions for their future.

Dave didn't have the tools to shift his mindset. But you do.

Through NLP, you can understand how your thoughts and words shape your reality, and how they influence the decisions of others. Whether you're in sales, leadership, or personal growth, mastering NLP and *Teach to Sell* gives you the ability to lead with impact.

Key Takeaways

- **Every choice leads to an outcome.** The way you sell, communicate, and lead determines your results.
- **Sales is about education, not persuasion.** *Teach to Sell* removes resistance by guiding people to clarity.
- **NLP helps you reshape your mindset—and your results.** When you understand how thoughts and language create reality, you can change your outcomes.
- **NLP techniques help guide decisions.** Embedded commands, tie-downs, future pacing, and reframing subtly direct clients toward favorable outcomes.

- **Trust is built through teaching.** Clients follow those who help them understand, not those who push them into a decision.

By committing to *Teach to Sell*, you ensure that every conversation moves your business and your clients in the right direction.

Commit or Quit Challenge: Are You Ready to Lead or Will You Let Others Decide for You?

There comes a moment in every journey when the hero is faced with a choice. Not just any choice, but *the* choice—the one that determines everything.

Dave had a choice. He could have rewritten his story, but he let his past dictate his future.

You have that same choice in sales and life.

Will you take full responsibility for guiding your clients? Will you step up as the leader they need? Or will you let someone else make the sale—someone less skilled, less ethical, or less committed than you?

This is your moment.

- Commit to mastering *Teach to Sell.*
- Commit to being the trusted expert.
- Commit to transforming your business and your life.

Or quit, and let someone else take your place.

The choice is yours.

Will you Commit or Quit?

CHAPTER 8

Teach to Communicate Effectively and Create Trust

THE LEADERSHIP LESSON I HAD TO LEARN THE HARD WAY

Owning the brokerage for five years, business was thriving. I had bought out toxic partners and most minority owners. Things were good, until they weren't.

The challenge? We had a CEO who was both brilliant and polarizing. She was dynamic, goal-driven, and unshakable in adversity. But her intensity made her seem unapproachable, shutting down alternative perspectives and creating a divide in the organization.

One day, after cleaning up yet another of her messes, I made a decision. I fired her.

What I didn't expect was the fallout.

The day after she was gone, an agent left. The next day, one of our top agents followed. One by one, they left, until it felt like a never-ending exodus. Each departure chipped away at my confidence. My thriving business was bleeding, and so was my self-worth.

That's when I learned one of the most painful but powerful lessons of my career: Communication determines everything.

I had failed to rally my agents before making a leadership change. The CEO I had fired had spent years influencing them, and in the absence of my own leadership, they followed her out

140

the door. I had expected loyalty but had not earned their trust through communication.

Through this, I learned that leadership isn't just about making decisions; it's about selling those decisions to others. It's about trust, clarity, and influence. And the foundation of all that is *Teach to Sell*.

HOW COMMUNICATION BECAME MY MOST VALUABLE SKILL

After a decade of owning the brokerage, I was at a crossroads. The business was being renovated, costing me hundreds of thousands of dollars.

Pacing back and forth in the unfinished space, I spoke with my coach, John.

John's guidance was clear: triple down on actions and recruit some big hitters.

But it felt too late. The cracks were already showing.

I learned the ropes of running a business in those first five years. The following five were a relentless struggle.

The turning point came when I was sitting in the office, surrounded by the half-finished build-out, facing a financial abyss.

I had already started the negotiations to sell to a new owner and made the decision. It was time.

I agreed to the price and terms of the buyer and notified the regional representative of the pending sale.

The Regional Operating Partner informed me I needed to write a resignation letter. Besides being the controlling owner, I also held an official role within the franchise that required resignation.

Thus, I composed the letter, scanned it into the overpriced printing machine we leased, signed it, and dispatched it to the Regional OP.

That marked the end of the communication between the Regional OP and me. It pained me profoundly that she never reached out or responded to my attempts to reconnect, especially considering the dedication I had shown to the franchisor.

With that, my identity as an Operating Partner came to an end.

Reflecting on my past, I now see how I allowed the label of "Operating Partner"—one of around 450 roles in an organization of approximately 180,000 people—to define me.

Identifying as an Operating Partner fed my ego and kept me entrenched in a role and business that wasn't benefiting me.

But through the experience described above, I discovered a profound truth: My true worth was not my title or position. It lay in my actions, my perception of myself, and my role as a dad.

My "aha" moment came when I realized I still had to fight. I didn't know the way but knew I could find it. It was my darkest hour in business, but it led to a breakthrough.

Before handing the business to the buyer, I wanted the agents who worked for me to know they would be in good hands and were safe. I spoke one-on-one with each person in the brokerage.

I understood that better communication was the key to ensuring others felt truly heard. This insight was life-changing.

Teach to Sell became my guiding light, and I discovered the **Consistent and Predictable Income (CPI)** Communication Model. It showed me the power of clear, empathetic communication.

I learned that I could build trust and lead effectively by teaching others.

Each step forward, every obstacle, was a chance to prove my worth and embrace my true potential.

PRE-DECISION COMPASS: THE FOUNDATION OF INFLUENCE

Before you engage in any sales conversation or leadership interaction, ask yourself:

- Am I entering this conversation with a focus on connection rather than persuasion?
- Have I considered the other person's emotional drivers and concerns?
- Am I prepared to listen more than I speak?
- Have I created an environment where trust can thrive?

PRE-DECISION TO MAKE

Commit to approaching every interaction with the intent to teach, guide, and empower. By prioritizing trust over transactions, you lay the foundation for influence and long-term success.

THE MEANING OF COMMUNICATION

> Communication is the response that you get.

Every conversation you have is filtered through a person's unique experiences, including:

- Values
- Beliefs
- Language
- Experience
- Education
- Culture
- Memories

We don't just hear words—we interpret them through our lens. That's why two people can hear the same thing but understand it completely differently.

To influence, sell, and lead effectively, you must communicate in a way that ensures your message is *received* as you intended.

HOW DO YOU DEFINE COMMUNICATION?

Have you ever interpreted something than what another meant to say?

Did you say or think,

"That is not what I said."

Take responsibility that their perception is as valid as yours.

You may be asking the wrong question if you request something from someone and do not get it.

EFFECTIVE COMMUNICATION IS MORE THAN JUST TALKING

Life coach Tony Robbins says,

> "To effectively communicate, we must realize that we are all different in the way we perceive the world and use this understanding as a guide to our communication with others."
> (Robbins, 1991)

Most sales trainers hand out scripts and tell you *what* to say. But very few teach you *why* it works (or doesn't).

Teach to Sell isn't about reciting words; it's about creating connection and trust. It's about guiding your clients to clarity so they can make the best decision for themselves.

To communicate effectively, ask yourself:

- Am I ensuring they feel heard?
- Am I focusing on their needs, not just my own message?
- Am I adapting my approach based on their responses?

Sales, leadership, and relationships are all built on how well you listen, not just how well you talk.

HOW CAN YOU BEST MAKE A CONNECTION WITH OTHER PEOPLE?

Understanding how communication works is like deciphering a secret code to connect better with others. The more you grasp its nuances, the smoother your ability to sway others.

Professor Albert Mehrabian's research, starting in the 1960s, has been a game-changer in understanding how we convey feelings and attitudes. His research (Mehrabian, 1967) suggests:

- Only 7 **percent** of how we express feelings and attitudes comes from our words.
- **Thirty-eight percent** comes from how we say things— our tone, pitch, and intonation.
- **Fifty-five percent** comes from our facial expressions because sometimes a smile speaks louder than words.

Remember, communication isn't just about what you say; it's also about the energy you convey and the vibes you pick up from others. It's a dance of words and feelings.

THE CPI COMMUNICATION MODEL

The CPI Communication Model: A Three-Step Process to Influence and Lead

The CPI Communication Model is a powerful system for mastering sales conversations and leadership influence.

THE CPI COMMUNICATION MODEL

Step 1: Build Rapport

- Rapport isn't small talk; it's a connection of energy between two or more people.
- Match body language, tone, and energy to create instant trust.
- People like people who are like them. Use this to make them feel comfortable.

Step 2: Ask Adept Questions

- Guide the conversation by asking the right questions, not by talking more.
- Understand not just the logical reasons but the emotional reasons behind a decision.
- Example: A divorced dad buying a house isn't just looking for three bedrooms; he's trying to stay close to his kids. Understanding that changes how you sell.

Step 3: Actively Listen

- Listen with full attention. People can tell when you're just waiting to talk.
- Repeat back key points to ensure clarity and show you understand.
- The less you talk, the more you sell.

Mastering these three steps will transform the way you lead, sell, and build relationships.

THE POWER OF RAPPORT IN SALES

Rapport is the foundation of all successful sales conversations. If you want to influence, you must first connect.

How Do You Know When You've Built Rapport?

You'll feel it. The conversation flows easily, trust is established, and resistance drops.

How Do You Create Rapport?

To develop rapport, you must communicate in the other person's "language." Pay attention to:

- Their words, tonality, and voice pitch
- Their body language and posture—are they leaning in or pulling away?
- Their energy—do they seem engaged or disconnected?

Rapport makes people feel comfortable, and comfort leads to trust.

Quick Hacks to Develop Rapport (A Connection of Energy)

Rapport can be built quickly with techniques like mirroring and matching.

- **Mirroring:** If they cross their arms, you cross yours.
- **Matching:** If they lean forward, you lean forward.
- **Crossover Matching:** Match their rhythm with a different movement, like tapping your pen in sync with their speech pattern.

Other techniques include:

- Match breathing patterns.
- Use similar gestures and posture.
- Speak their language—literally and figuratively.

- Maintain eye contact (without making it awkward).
- Smile (a reminder I often need myself!).
- Ask open-ended questions.

When you build rapport, you create trust. When you create trust, you gain influence.

Can More Than One Person Be in Rapport at the Same Time?

Absolutely. Think of a restaurant staff moving in sync during a busy dinner rush. They barely look at each other but never collide because they have rapport.

The same principle applies in sales and leadership. You can create rapport with an entire group by tuning into the room's energy.

STEP 2: ASK ADEPT QUESTIONS

Adept questions are powerful. They:

- Prompt deeper reflection
- Encourage open communication
- Reveal emotional motivators behind decisions

Understanding Your Client's Emotional Experience

Most salespeople only focus on surface needs. But the best salespeople dig deeper.

Example: Imagine you are a real estate agent and a client says they need a three-bedroom house near work.

- **Good salesperson:** "Got it, let's find a three-bedroom near your job."

- **CPI salesperson (skilled in *Teach to Sell*)**: "Tell me more. Why is being close to work important?"

If you dig deeper, you may learn that he just went through a divorce and fears losing time with his kids. **Now, you're not just selling a house—you're helping him preserve his role as a father.**

People buy based on emotion and justify with logic. Uncover their real motivation, and you'll guide them to the right decision.

Common emotional states of buyers and sellers:

- Nervous about relocating
- Anxious about money
- Worried about their kids' school
- Stressed about relationships
- Sentimentally attached to a home

Your job is to understand their emotional landscape and guide them through it.

STEP 3: ACTIVE LISTENING

In the **CPI Communication Model**, Step 1 establishes rapport, Step 2 asks the right questions, and Step 3 ensures you actually hear the answers.

How to Display Active Listening

Follow this pattern:

1. Ask a question.
2. Listen to the response.
3. Repeat back what you heard.
4. Pause. Silence creates space for deeper thoughts.

5. Hear their next response before moving forward.

6. Observe the energy of the other person

Strategic listening gives you control of the conversation while making the other person feel heard.

TALK LESS. SELL MORE.

Many salespeople think they need to talk a lot to prove their expertise. The opposite is true.

- The best salespeople say less and listen more.
- Clients will tell you exactly how to sell to them—if you let them talk.
- Your role is to guide, not dominate.

Example: I once had a salesperson on my team who wouldn't stop talking.

He was confident but rarely closed deals. Why? Because he never gave prospects a chance to tell him what they needed.

Asking questions and listening don't just help in sales; it transforms your relationships, leadership, and personal growth.

APPLYING THE CPI COMMUNICATION MODEL IN REAL LIFE

Mastering rapport, asking adept questions, and actively listening isn't just theory; it's the foundation of *Teach to Sell*.

By applying these skills consistently, you:

- Build trust effortlessly.
- Guide clients to the best decisions.
- Remove resistance from sales conversations.

These aren't just sales techniques; they are *life skills* that lead to better relationships, leadership, and success.

But communication isn't just about *what* you say; it's also about *how* you say it.

HIERARCHY OF COMMUNICATION

The Power of Communication Mediums

Not all communication methods are created equal. The impact of your message depends on how you deliver it.

Hierarchy of Communication (Most Effective to Least Effective)

1. **Face-to-face**—The top standard for connection, trust, and influence.
2. **Video calls (Zoom, FaceTime, and so on)**—Allows for visual cues but lacks physical presence.
3. **Phone calls**—Good for direct conversation but misses non-verbal elements.
4. **Text messages**—Convenient, but easy to misinterpret tone.
5. **Social media messages**—Good for engagement but lacks depth.
6. **Emails**—Great for documentation but impersonal and often ignored.

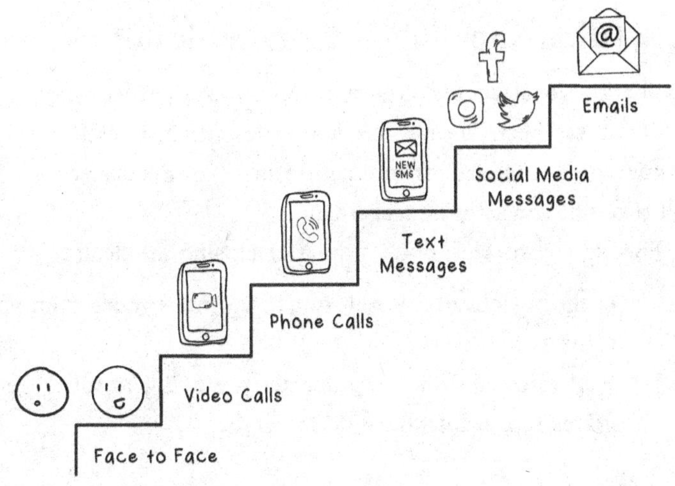

Whenever possible, **choose the highest-impact communication method.** Texts and emails leave too much room for misinterpretation. If the conversation matters, make it personal.

Why Overcommunication Is a Competitive Advantage

Some fear overcommunicating, thinking it might annoy clients. The truth? Lack of communication is what loses deals.

When my daughter attended Montessori Preschool, I received updates every few days—emails, texts, and phone calls. I never had to wonder how she was doing. When we moved and she started a new school, the communication dropped to near zero. The quality of education may have been the same, but my confidence in the school plummeted.

The same principle applies in business. Clients trust the professional who keeps them informed. Overcommunication isn't excessive; it's a competitive advantage.

How Often Should You Communicate?

If you want loyal clients, communicate more than expected. My sales team connects with each client at least five times per week. We guarantee this level of interaction in writing because trust is built through consistent engagement.

For big-ticket sales, don't stop after closing the deal:

- **Ongoing clients:** Reach out three times more than you think is necessary.
- **Past clients:** Follow up quarterly. Staying in touch generates repeat business and referrals.

Why Frequent Communication Prevents Problems

Regular communication acts as a buffer. When challenges arise, clients who feel consistently engaged are less likely to blame you. Studies confirm this:

- Regular check-ins strengthen relationships and reduce misunderstandings. (Stafford, 1991)
- Clients who feel engaged are less likely to assign blame during difficulties. (Davidow, Organizational responses to customer complaints: What works and what doesn't. , 2003)
- Satisfied clients are more likely to refer business. (Reichheld & Sasser, 1990)

Teach to Sell Exercise: Mastering Trust Through Communication

Think of a past client interaction where you faced resistance. Answer these questions:

1. How well did you build rapport before introducing your offer?

    ____

    ____

    ____

    ____

2. Did you uncover the client's real emotional trigger, or did you stay at surface level?

    ____

    ____

    ____

    ____

3. How much did you listen versus talk? Did you let the client fully express their thoughts?

    ____

    ____

    ____

    ____

4. If you had used the **CPI Communication Model**, how might the outcome have changed?

    ____

    ____

    ____

    ____

Now, apply this to your next client conversation. Set a goal to focus more on listening, uncovering deep motivations, and mirroring their communication style.

COMMIT OR QUIT CHALLENGE: WILL YOU MASTER COMMUNICATION OR KEEP LOSING INFLUENCE?

Every deal, every negotiation, every leadership moment hinges on communication. **If you don't master it, someone else will.**

Will you commit to mastering the **CPI Communication Model**—building rapport, asking adept questions, and actively listening?

Or will you keep guessing, losing deals, and struggling to influence others?

The choice is yours.

Commit to *Teach to Sell*, and you'll never look at communication the same way again.

Will you Commit or Quit?

Part II

GENERATE LEADS

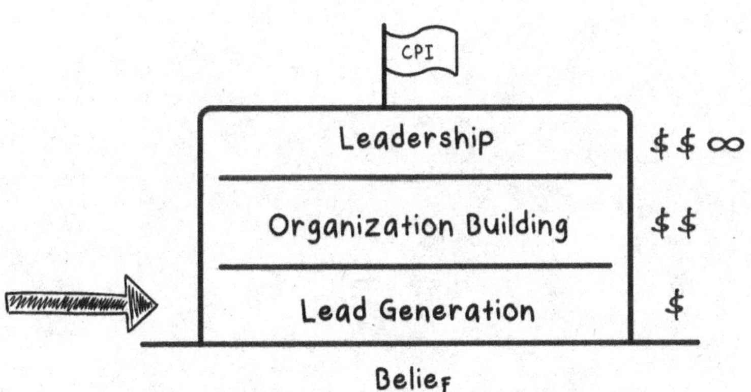

CHAPTER 9

Teach to Find Business

FACING THE FEAR THAT WASN'T REAL

I was forty-nine, lying awake most of the night, heart pounding.

How would I tell my daughter Maggie that her mom and I were getting a divorce?

I doubted it would surprise my twelve-year-old—after all, I had been sleeping in the guest room for over a year.

Maggie means everything to me. I put her above all else, except my sobriety. My wife and I had agreed to divorce a year prior, and all the details were settled. But telling Maggie—that final step—terrified me more than anything.

Would I break her heart? Would I repeat the painful patterns of my own childhood? Would she still feel loved?

Meanwhile, my business had returned to thriving after a rough stretch. My wife and I had presented a unified front to the public and the marketplace for years. While I resented the inauthenticity, we had done what we felt was best.

Now, it was time to tell Maggie.

Finally, Traci and I sat down outside with her, and I took the lead.

As gently as possible, I said,

"Maggie, I love you. Your mom and I are getting a divorce."

She looked at me and said,

"OK."

I asked,

"Are you OK?"

She said,

"Yes. I love you and Mommy."

I had built up this moment in my head for so long, dreading the pain it would bring her. Yet, as best as I could tell, she was fine.

And the relief was overwhelming.

THE BUSINESS LESSON: FEAR HOLDS US BACK

I share this story because sometimes, in life and business, fear holds us hostage. But often, what we fear most isn't real. The biggest obstacles are not external—they exist in our minds.

How many times have you delayed lead generation because of fear?

- Fear of rejection
- Fear of sounding salesy
- Fear of hearing "no"

But what if you discovered that, just like Maggie was fine, your business will thrive if you take action?

TEACH TO SELL STRATEGY

Instead of fearing outreach, teach your prospects. Every conversation is an opportunity to add value, share insights, and position yourself as the expert.

When you shift from selling to teaching, fear disappears. It's because you're not pushing something on people; you're helping them get what they already want.

PRE-DECISION COMPASS: OVERCOMING FEAR TO TAKE ACTION

Before you begin lead generation, reflect:

- What fear is holding me back from taking action?
- What's the worst that could happen if I fail? What's the best that could happen if I succeed?
- What would my business look like ninety days from now if I *consistently* took action?
- How would I feel knowing I've built unstoppable momentum?

PRE-DECISION TO MAKE

Say to yourself,

> "I will commit to daily lead generation, knowing that consistency creates success."

THE POWER OF BOLD ACTION

Have You Ever Put Off Something Important Because of Fear?

The longer you wait, the bigger the fear grows. But once you take action, you realize it wasn't nearly as bad as you imagined.

We hesitate to make bold moves because we fear failure or rejection. But those same bold moves are often what create our biggest breakthroughs.

It's like when I told Maggie about the divorce. The fear was overwhelming, but once I faced it, I felt free.

Applying This to Business

Think about a time in business when fear held you back. Maybe it was:

- Launching a new service
- Raising your prices
- Reaching out to a big client

Doubt made you hesitate. But what if taking that step led to unexpected success?

Just like Maggie was OK, you might find that bold action in business opens doors you never expected.

Embrace the Unexpected

Often, the path we fear most leads to the greatest rewards. Imagine turning fear into triumph, both in business and life.

Take that bold step. Make the daring move. Watch your world expand in ways you never imagined.

Success often comes from doing things that feel uncomfortable at first.

Think about those potential clients you've been afraid to contact. Reach out. Show them your passion and expertise. Despite your nerves, they could become your most loyal customers.

Consider strategies that seem risky or unconventional.

Learn from Richard Branson

Richard Branson built Virgin Group by challenging the norm.

When he launched Virgin Atlantic, he made air travel exciting—onboard bars, better entertainment, and a focus on customer experience.

He took the same bold approach in music, telecom, and even space travel. His success wasn't about playing it safe. It was about taking chances and putting people first.

Branson's story proves that unconventional moves can lead to extraordinary results.

So, dare to try new marketing strategies. Collaborate with competitors. Take the leap. These fearless moves can set you apart and fuel your growth.

Take the First Step

Success starts with a single step. Find your first move and build momentum from there. The sooner you take action, the faster you'll see new opportunities unfold.

What bold step will you take today?

THE FLYWHEEL EFFECT: TURN EFFORT INTO UNSTOPPABLE SUCCESS

Picture a massive steel flywheel, sitting idle on its shaft. It's almost impossible to move. Your job? Get it turning.

You plant your feet, lean in, and push. Nothing happens. You push again, still nothing. The weight of it is overwhelming.

But you don't stop. Sweat beads on your forehead as you throw your entire body into the effort. A tiny shift. The wheel moves, barely.

You keep pushing. Inch by inch, it turns. Then, something changes. One full rotation. Then another. And another. Soon, the wheel is spinning so fast it seems unstoppable.

Now, ask yourself:

Was it the first push that made the difference? Or the last?

It doesn't matter. The truth is, if you had stopped at any point before the flywheel gained momentum, all your effort would have been wasted. You would have had to start over, losing all progress and returning to zero.

Your sales career works the same way.

NO BROKE MONTHS START WITH ONE PUSH

So, how do you create No Broke Months?

The answer is consistency.

Small actions, repeated daily, compound into unstoppable momentum. Just like the flywheel, success in business starts slow.

At first, you see little to no return. It's frustrating. But if you stay committed, tiny results start stacking up. Those tiny results turn into big ones.

And suddenly, you're not chasing success anymore, it's chasing you.

THE #1 HABIT OF TOP SALESPEOPLE

When coaching salespeople, I always start with two questions:

1. What are your goals?
2. Do you currently have enough business to hit those goals?

If the answer to #2 is "no," then there is only one thing you should focus on: finding more business.

Because here's the truth—if you have *no* business, you have *no* business doing anything else but *finding* business.

Imagine having an overflow of opportunities. Picture being able to choose the clients you work with and how you spend your time. That freedom comes from one thing: consistently generating leads.

THE COMPOUND EFFECT OF DAILY LEAD GENERATION

> You are in the lead generation business,
>
> specializing in sales in the niche of your industry.

What if you dedicated just one to three hours *every* workday to finding new business?

At first, it might not seem like much. But over time, that effort compounds into something powerful, a pipeline so strong that your business never slows down.

This is where most people fail. They lead-generate inconsistently, pushing their flywheel forward a little...then stopping. Then, when they need clients, they scramble to start over.

Don't be that person.

Be *unshakable* in your commitment.

Lead generation is not optional, it's the foundation of your entire business.

THE FORMULA FOR NO BROKE MONTHS

Want a consistent and predictable business? Follow this formula:

1. Lead generate for one to three hours every workday. Five days a week. No excuses.
2. Do it first thing in the morning. When you have the most energy and the fewest distractions.
3. Know what lead generation really is. It's not just about today's sales, it's about filling your pipeline for the future.

Lead generation is *the art* of creating opportunities. It's about consistently connecting with people, guiding them through the process, and ensuring that when they're ready to buy, you're the one they call.

Master this, and you'll never have another broke month again.

So, what's your next move?

Are you pushing the flywheel today, or letting it stop?

What results should you expect from your efforts?

Your outcomes will depend on:
- How often do you say it?
- What are you saying?
- Who are you saying it to?.

HOW OFTEN ARE YOU SAYING IT?

Most successful salespeople generate leads each workday. On average, they speak with ten to twenty people about their product or service daily.

Less successful salespeople will prospect sporadically or start, stop, and decide that prospecting does not work. They will get rejected by a prospect and then cease the activity.

If you intend to be successful, select how many people you will speak with each day and do the activity without fail.

WHAT ARE YOU SAYING?

Mastering Objections: The Secret to Closing More Deals

How Do You Know What to Say When You Receive an Objection?

If you're doing your job right as a salesperson, objections should become less frequent. Why? Because great salespeople don't just react to objections, they prevent them before they ever arise.

When you deeply understand your client's priorities, you can anticipate concerns and address them upfront. But even the best sales strategies can't eliminate every single objection. So, when one does surface, the way you handle it determines whether you win the deal—or lose it.

Can You Avoid Every Objection?

Even with perfect execution, objections can still appear. But here's what separates top closers from everyone else: They don't get blindsided by objections, they welcome them.

Why? Because objections mean the prospect is engaged. They're thinking about what you're offering. And if they're engaged, you have an opportunity.

The Real Risk of Unresolved Objections

If a prospect walks away from a conversation still holding onto objections, your chances of getting hired shrink dramatically. Worse, if they're confused or hesitant throughout the process, it's a sign that your presentation isn't landing.

The good news? There's a proven method to uncover and eliminate objections before they derail your deal.

The Formula to Handle Any Objection

Want to know the one simple question that can uncover hidden objections?

"What would stop you from moving forward?"

It's direct. It's powerful. And it forces the prospect to lay their cards on the table.

Once they share an objection, use this three-step process to turn it into an opportunity:

1. **Repeat and affirm.** Acknowledge their concern and validate their thinking.
2. **Isolate the objection.** Make sure no other hidden objections exist.
3. **Handle the objection.** Address the real issue head-on.

HOW THIS WORKS IN ACTION

Imagine a prospect raises a concern. Here's how you handle it:

1. Repeat and Affirm

Prospect:

> "I'm not sure about moving forward."

Salesperson:

> "I hear you. That's a smart way to approach a
> decision like this."

You're making them feel understood. You're positioning them as thoughtful and strategic, which lowers their defensiveness.

2. Isolate the Objection

Salesperson:

> "Other than that, is there anything else stop-
> ping you from moving forward today?"

This ensures you're dealing with the real issue, not just a surface-level excuse.

3. Handle the Objection

Once the true concern is out in the open, you can address it confidently.

HANDLING THE MOST COMMON OBJECTION: "I HAVE TO THINK ABOUT IT"

This is the ultimate smokescreen. When a prospect says this, it usually means they're hesitant about something deeper. Here's how to get to the root of it:

Option 1: Dig Deeper

Prospect:

"I have to think about it."

Salesperson:

"You have to think about it? That's smart—you want to make the right decision." (Repeat and affirm)

Salesperson:

"Other than that, is there anything else holding you back?" (Isolate the objection)

Prospect:

"No, that's it."

Salesperson:

"Got it. Out of curiosity, what specifically do you need to think about?" (Handle the objection)

Now, the real concern comes to the surface, and you can address it directly.

Option 2: Get Them Talking

Prospect:

"I have to think about it."

Salesperson:

"Tell me more about that."

That simple phrase encourages them to reveal their true hesitation, giving you the insight you need to close the deal.

TURN OBJECTIONS INTO OPPORTUNITIES

Every objection is a chance to build trust, provide clarity, and guide the prospect toward a confident decision. Mastering this process won't just help you close more deals, it will make you the kind of salesperson people want to buy from.

Will you apply this strategy in your next conversation, or will you let objections keep costing you sales?

WHO ARE YOU SAYING IT TO?

As a business owner, pinpointing the right audience is paramount when communicating the value of your product or service. Crafting messages tailored to resonate with those most likely to benefit ensures that your efforts are targeted and effective.

By clearly defining the individuals or businesses most likely to benefit from your product or service, you can tailor your marketing efforts and communication to resonate with their needs and preferences.

TEACH A PERSON TO FISH, AND YOU FEED THEM FOR A LIFETIME

The Alaska Fishing Trip: Lessons from a Novice Angler

When my father turned sixty-five, I took him on a salmon fishing trip to Alaska.

I had never fished for salmon before. But there I was, on the legendary Kenai River, trolling for king salmon.

Getting Ready for the Catch

As a beginner, I knew I needed help. So, I hired a guide and asked the captain every question I could think of.

Early in the morning, we got to work. First, we checked our gear—bait, rods, rigs, and everything else we needed. Then, we made sure our hooks were razor-sharp. Salmon have tough jaws, and a dull hook wouldn't cut it.

Choosing the Right Strategy

There were several ways to catch salmon, and we had to pick wisely:

- **Trolling with a lure**—A classic method.
- **Flossing**—Casting a baitless hook upstream and letting it drift into the salmon's mouth.
- **Drift fishing**—Similar to flossing but with bait.
- **Plunking**—Anchoring bait in the salmon's path, waiting for them to strike.
- **Bobber fishing**—A backup plan when nothing else worked.

For bait, we tried different options, but roe (fish eggs) worked best.

Timing Matters

It wasn't just about the method—it was about the moment. Salmon follow a seasonal rhythm. The mighty King Salmon moves from the ocean to the river to spawn from early June to early July.

The best time to fish? The hour before or after high or low tide. That was the window for the perfect catch.

In fishing, just like in life, having the right tools, asking the right questions, and knowing when to act makes all the difference (McClane, 1978)

Lead Generation Is Like Fishing

Why tell you about my fishing trip? Because lead generation works the same way.

To catch salmon, we needed patience, the right tools, and the right strategy. To succeed in lead generation, you need the same.

How to Catch More Clients
(Just Like Fish)

Get a Guide

Prepare Your Approach

Sharpen Your Hooks (Skills)

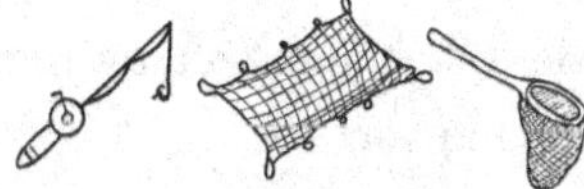

Choose Your Strategy

Fish When They're Biting

HOW TO CATCH MORE CLIENTS (JUST LIKE FISH)

Get a Guide

- Hire a coach or mentor.
- Ask them every question you can think of.

Prepare Your Approach

- Block your time.
- Know who you're contacting.
- Eliminate distractions.

Sharpen Your Hooks (Skills)

- Practice scripts.
- Master communication.
- Be ready to handle objections.

Choose Your Strategy

- How will you find clients? Cold calls? Social media? Networking?

Fish When They're Biting

- When are your prospects available?
- If you're door-knocking, Saturday mornings work better than Monday afternoons.

Sales, like fishing, should be fun. Make it a game, enjoy the process, and you'll have more energy, joy, and success.

WHERE DO LEADS COME FROM?

Bruce Lee once remarked,

> "I fear not the man who has practiced 10,000 kicks once, but I fear the man who has practiced one kick 10,000 times." (Lee, 1975)

This philosophy applies to lead generation. It's better to send 10,000 pieces of marketing mail to your most likely clients than one piece of mail to 10,000 people.

Moreover, success in any endeavor typically requires a minimum commitment of eighteen months to yield optimal results. Understanding these principles positions you for success.

The **Commit or Quit** concept is instrumental in understanding effective lead generation strategies.

You must fully commit to your actions to succeed in sales or any endeavor.

Understand your purpose behind making sales, decide on your approach, and dedicate yourself to that path until you achieve your desired results.

Commitment is the key that unlocks success.

There is no wrong way to get a lead. All lead generation techniques work when you fully commit to do them consistently.

As your business grows, consider adding additional sources.

TRANSACTIONAL VS. RELATIONAL MARKETING

What Is Transactional Marketing?

Transactional marketing means you work with people you have not yet met. You can do this through radio advertising, internet advertising, telemarketing, networking, other paid advertising, and other ways.

What Is Relational Marketing?

Relational marketing means you work with people you have met—or at least you had a conversation with.

Which Strategy Is Best: Transactional or Relational Marketing?

Consider using both methodologies.

Intend to meet many people through transactional marketing and then use relational marketing strategies to provide them excessive value and convert them into an advocate at a high level.

It is an intelligent strategy to focus on maintaining valuable relationships with those who you know. These people will be the moat around your business that protects outside influences and the evolution of sales from harming you.

The strength of your database represents the strength of your business. The larger your pool of people is, and the more systematically you contribute high value to those people, the more insulated your business shall be from threats.

To scale your business, you must cultivate those contacts you already know and create new ones through developing transactional connections into meaningful relationships.

Everyone you know today (except your mother) was a stranger to you. You met them, established a connection, and cultivated a relationship.

Your intention with transactional marketing should be to transform those people into your relational marketing system.

> **What are the broad ways to find clients?**
>
> You can find clients through marketing, prospecting, or networking.

Is There a Cost to Finding Business?

There is always a cost to everything you do. For example, marketing costs money, prospecting costs time, and networking costs both time and money.

Newer salespeople typically have more time than money. If this is the case, then choose prospecting.

Use one to three of the following tactics to identify the most promising individuals (those most likely to make a purchase) to engage in conversation: prospecting, networking, and marketing.

PROSPECTING

Mastering the Art of Prospecting

Prospecting isn't about chasing leads, it's about positioning yourself as the trusted guide who helps prospects achieve what they want. When done right, it builds long-term relationships, authority, and a consistent flow of clients.

Teach to Sell means leading prospects to their own conclusions through value-driven engagement. Let's explore high-impact prospecting methods to create **No Broke Months** in your business.

High-Impact Prospecting Methods

1. Cold Calling and Circle Prospecting

Direct conversations remain one of the fastest ways to generate business. Cold calling, when done with a strategic approach, can yield high returns. Be sure to comply with all Do Not Call regulations.

Teach to Sell **Strategy:** Approach cold calls as an opportunity to educate, not just sell. Ask discovery questions to help the prospect see the value in what you offer.

2. Referrals and Strategic Partnerships

Referrals are your best source of warm leads. Actively ask satisfied clients to refer you and form partnerships with complementary businesses.

Teach to Sell **Strategy:** Frame referral requests as a way for your clients to help others, rather than just helping you. Make it about serving, not selling.

3. Special Promotions

Limited-time offers create urgency and encourage immediate action. Bundle products or services to enhance perceived value.

Teach to Sell **Strategy:** Instead of pushing promotions, educate your audience on why the bundled offer solves their problem better than a single purchase.

4. Local Events and Sponsorships

Community involvement increases brand trust and credibility. Attend or sponsor local events to connect with potential clients.

Teach to Sell **Strategy**: Engage with event attendees by teaching them something valuable. Give actionable insights instead of just promoting your business.

5. Customer Feedback and Reviews

Positive testimonials are one of the most powerful forms of social proof. Encourage happy clients to leave online reviews.

Teach to Sell **Strategy**: Feature testimonials in a storytelling format. Show the transformation your service created rather than just stating praise.

6. Strategic Alliances and Joint Ventures

Partner with non-competing businesses that serve the same audience to expand your reach.

Teach to Sell **Strategy**: Frame alliances as a way to provide more value to both your audiences. Co-create content or host joint events to leverage each other's trust and credibility.

7. Optimize Your Online Presence

Your website and social media should attract and nurture leads without requiring continuous effort.

- **SEO Optimization:** Rank for terms your audience searches for.
- **Blog Consistency:** Establish credibility by publishing educational content regularly.
- **Video Marketing:** Leverage video to engage and convert prospects.

- **Active Social Media Presence:** Use platforms like Facebook to nurture relationships.

Teach to Sell **Strategy:** Create content that shifts mindsets. Don't just inform—transform.

8. YouTube Hack for Massive Reach

- **Optimize Your Video**: Use an eye-catching thumbnail, SEO-friendly title, and an engaging hook within five seconds.
- **Go Live**: The algorithm favors live content.
- **Leverage Your Email List**: Send your database a direct link immediately after posting.
- **Boost with Ads**: A small ad spend (five dollars a day for seven days) can significantly increase views and engagement.

Using this system, I consistently generate three thousand to five thousand views per video.

Teach to Sell **Strategy:** Follow the blueprint (please like and subscribe) at www.youtube.com/NoBrokeMonths.

9. Facebook Hack

- **Build Connections**: Send friend requests to your ideal audience.
- **Engage Before Selling**: Comment and interact meaningfully.
- **Post Using the 4:1 Ratio**: Four personal posts for every educational or business post.

Teach to Sell **Strategy:** Use stories to illustrate problems and solutions rather than just stating facts.

10. Content Marketing for Authority

- **Create Valuable Content**: Share insights through blogs, videos, and podcasts.
- **Promote Across Platforms**: Don't just post—strategically distribute.
- **Analyze Competitors**: Study what works and fill in market gaps.

Teach to Sell **Strategy**: Make your content a conversation, not a lecture.

11. Educational and Charity Events for Visibility

Hosting events isn't just about showing up—it's about positioning yourself as the trusted authority in your industry. Whether it's an educational workshop or a charity-driven event, the goal is to create meaningful engagement that builds credibility and generates leads.

Teach to Sell **Strategy**: Use storytelling to create emotional connections. Don't just share information—frame it in a way that shows attendees how to think differently about their problems and your solution. The more you help them shift their mindset, the more they'll trust you to guide them toward success.

12. Workshops and Webinars

Virtual and in-person workshops are high-value lead magnets that allow you to demonstrate expertise while engaging your audience. Live Q&As build credibility and make your brand more accessible.

- Teach industry-specific solutions to common problems.
- Answer audience questions live to create engagement.

Teach to Sell **Strategy:** Lead with value and end with a clear next step. Start by solving a small but urgent problem your audience faces. This builds trust and positions you as the go-to expert. Then, seamlessly transition into an offer that helps them solve the bigger problem with your paid service or product.

13. Charity Events

Aligning your brand with a cause boosts trust, goodwill, and local visibility. People want to do business with those who share their values.

Teach to Sell **Strategy:** Connect the cause with your audience's deeper motivations. For example, a Title Company owner I coach hosts monthly paid events, using the proceeds to support local charities. Not only does this position her as a community leader, but it also attracts like-minded clients who value social impact.

For another example, a mortgage broker could host a "Homes for Heroes" event, offering insights on real-estate financing while supporting first responders or veterans. The goodwill generated translates into long-term loyalty and referrals.

14. Other Event Success Stories

A youth entrepreneurship program leader I coach saw massive exposure after hosting an expo. The result? Media coverage worth tens of thousands in free publicity.

Teach to Sell **Strategy:** Use events to educate and inspire action. Don't just promote—position yourself as the guide to transformation.

Your Challenge

Choose three prospecting strategies from this guide and commit to them for the next thirty days. Track your results, refine your approach, and scale what works. Are you ready to create **No Broke Months**?

By integrating *Teach to Sell* into your prospecting efforts, you shift from pushing to pulling—attracting and converting leads with authority and trust.

NETWORKING

> Networking is a strategy that allows
> you to leverage your time.
>
> Consider this as an approach of One to Many.

The Power of Networking: How *Teach to Sell* Transforms Connections into Success

In 2007, I was a brand-new real estate agent with no established network. In an industry driven by referrals and relationships, I faced an uphill battle. I had no pipeline, no connections, and no idea where my next deal would come from.

But I refused to let that stop me.

I thought back to my father's success in business and how he leveraged networking groups to expand his reach. Seeking guidance, I turned to him, and he pointed me to Business Network International (BNI), a community of professionals who exchange referrals and support one another.

Excited by the opportunity, I quickly reached out to the local BNI representative, Juli. But instead of a warm welcome, she shut me down:

"Joining an existing group isn't an option for a newcomer like you."

I guess Juli didn't understand my relationship with **Commit or Quit**—and quitting was never on the table.

Instead of backing down, I asked,

"How do I start my own group?"

Juli laughed, but she saw my determination. She challenged me to read *Givers Gain: The BNI Story*, visit two active BNI chapters, and complete a series of assignments.

Challenge accepted.

I completed every task swiftly and founded **BNI Positive Power**—my own networking group. For the next six months, I poured in forty hours a week, recruiting members, organizing meetings, and building a powerhouse community.

For seventeen years, I showed up early every Wednesday morning to foster relationships with entrepreneurs committed to growing their businesses. Though I am no longer a member, BNI Positive Power continues to thrive because of the foundation I built.

That's the real power of networking: creating something bigger than yourself. It is something that lives on even when you step away.

Networking Is a *Teach to Sell* Strategy

Networking isn't about showing up and asking for business. It's about creating value for others first. The secret? *Teach to Sell.* Show others how to think in ways that help them achieve their goals, and they'll naturally want to follow your lead.

The Right Way to Network

Most people think networking means finding people who can help you. But the most successful networkers do the opposite.

They focus on helping others first.

Imagine you're a real estate agent at a networking event. You meet:

- A baker
- An auto mechanic
- A carpet installation professional

Who Should You Prioritize Building a Relationship With?

The carpet installer.

Why? Because you sell homes, and your clients often need carpet replacement. By referring business to them, you become valuable. Over time, that value comes back to you—tenfold.

For example, as a real estate agent, I built a relationship with a landscaping contractor simply because I liked him and knew I could easily send him referrals. Over time, he returned the favor— resulting in over **$150,000 in additional income for me.**

How to Gain an Edge in Networking

To succeed in networking, **build relationships strategically.** Ask yourself:

- Who can I genuinely help first?
- How can I add value to this person's business?
- What connections do I already have that might benefit them?
- Who in my network would benefit from knowing them?

When you make others successful, they will naturally want to do the same for you. That's the *Teach to Sell* advantage.

Networking is not just about collecting business cards. It's about becoming a trusted, valuable resource in your industry.

Here's your challenge:

1. Attend a networking event this week.
2. Identify three people you can help.
3. Make at least one referral to someone in your network.
4. Follow up and offer additional value.

Where to Network: A List of High-Value Opportunities

Ready to expand your network? Consider these options:

- Business Network International
- Chamber of Commerce events
- Meetups (Meetup.com)
- Toastmasters
- Industry conferences and trade shows
- Charity and volunteer opportunities
- Cultural and civic organizations
- Sporting clubs
- Parent groups (PTA, local community groups)

Building a High-Value Network for Consistent Sales

Success in sales isn't just about closing deals, it's about building relationships that create a steady flow of business. The best sales professionals don't just work their network; they train their network to work for them. They make it easy for referral partners, past clients, and even prospects to think of them first when an opportunity arises.

If you want to create a predictable stream of opportunities, start by educating the people who can send you business. Most salespeople assume their network understands how to refer them, but in reality, most don't. The solution is simple: **Give them this book.**

Here's what to do next: Order five extra copies and hand them to the people who have the most potential to send you leads.

Tell them,

> "This is how I think about sales. The more
> you understand my approach, the easier it is
> for us to win together."

Whether you're working with a referral partner, a key prospect, or a sales team that needs a proven system, equipping others with the right mindset helps you build momentum.

The most successful salespeople don't just sell. They educate, they influence, and they create systems that multiply their efforts. This book isn't just for you—it's for the people who can help you succeed.

Final Thought: *Teach to Sell* and Win at Networking

When you shift your mindset from "What can I get" to "How can I help," you unlock the real power of networking.

Step out of your comfort zone. Build connections. Share your expertise.

And watch as opportunities flow your way effortlessly.

MARKETING

If you've been successful in sales for a while and have money to invest, it's time to consider marketing.

Why? Because prospecting alone has limits; your time is finite. When you hit that ceiling, the only way to scale is to market.

The right marketing strategy will work alongside your prospecting efforts, allowing you to attract clients even when you're not actively hunting for them.

Before diving in, ask yourself:

- Have I maximized my prospecting efforts and hit a time constraint?
- Do I have the financial resources to invest without jeopardizing my business stability?
- Am I ready to track and optimize my marketing results for maximum return on investment?
- What marketing strategies align best with my strengths and target audience?

If your time is fully booked with prospecting, marketing is your next step to grow your business predictably.

How to Market: Paid Strategies for Business Growth

Marketing is an investment. When done correctly, it generates a steady flow of high-quality leads, freeing you from the constant cycle of cold outreach.

The key is to select marketing methods that align with your strengths, so you execute them with confidence and consistency. Below are powerful ways to market using paid methods.

Online Advertising

- **Google Ads**: Appear at the top of search results when potential clients search for relevant terms.
- **Social Media Ads**: Target specific demographics and interests on platforms like Facebook, Instagram, LinkedIn, and X (Twitter).
- **Display Advertising**: Place banner ads on high-traffic websites that your target audience visits.
- **Content Syndication**: Pay to distribute your content across popular websites to expand your reach.
- **Email Marketing**: Use targeted email lists and invest in sponsored newsletters to directly reach potential clients.
- **Lead Generation Services**: Purchase warm leads from companies specializing in lead acquisition.
- **Influencer Marketing**: Partner with industry influencers to promote your business to their audience.
- **Affiliate Marketing**: Pay affiliates a commission for referring new customers to you.
- **Sponsorships**: Sponsor events, podcasts, or industry conferences for brand visibility.
- **Webinars and Workshops**: Host educational events and use paid ads to attract the right attendees.
- **Direct Mail Marketing**: Send personalized, high-value mailers to a carefully selected audience.
- **Lead Magnets**: Create free resources (ebooks, guides, templates) and promote them with paid ads to capture leads.
- **Pay-Per-Lead Services**: Pay only for qualified leads instead of impressions or clicks.
- **Retargeting Ads**: Re-engage website visitors who didn't convert by showing them targeted ads.

- **LinkedIn Premium**: Access advanced search filters and message high-value prospects directly.
- **Paid Spokespeople**: Hire credible figures to endorse your products and boost brand trust.

To be successful, you need to understand your audience's pain points. Speak directly to their challenges and position yourself as the solution.

Effective marketing isn't just about showing up, it's about making a meaningful connection that moves people to action.

Trade Shows and Exhibitions

Invest in booth space to showcase your services to a highly targeted audience. Face-to-face interactions at these events can convert to high-quality leads.

Old-School Advertising

While digital marketing is dominant, traditional media still has power, especially for local branding:

- **Radio Ads**: Engage commuters and local audiences with audio marketing.
- **Television Ads**: Build credibility with high-production TV commercials.
- **Billboards**: Capture attention with high-visibility placements in key locations.

New Ways to Use Old-School Advertising for Maximum Impact

Traditional advertising still holds value, but smart marketers are using digital tools to amplify its reach and effectiveness.

Instead of spending massive budgets on physical ads with limited targeting, you can now leverage digital versions of these classic methods to reach the right audience at the right time—without wasting dollars on the wrong market.

Podcast Advertising: The New Radio

Podcast advertising allows you to reach highly targeted audiences based on interests, demographics, and listening habits. Unlike traditional radio, where ads are broadcast to a general audience, podcast ads are placed in niche shows with engaged listeners.

How to Advertise on Podcasts

- Use platforms like Spotify Ad Studio, AdvertiseCast, or Podbean to place ads on podcasts.
- Target based on category, such as business, real estate, finance, wellness, and so on.
- Choose host-read ads for more trust and engagement.
- Create dynamic ad insertion campaigns to reach fresh listeners over time.

This method ensures your message reaches an audience that wants to hear it, rather than just hoping someone tunes in at the right moment.

Hulu and Streaming Services: The New Television Ads

With more people cutting cable and switching to streaming, services like Hulu, YouTube TV, and Roku offer a smarter way to do TV advertising. Unlike traditional TV, where you pay for airtime with little control over who sees your ad, streaming platforms let you target specific viewers based on location, interests, and even behavior.

How to Advertise on Hulu and Streaming Services:

- Use Hulu Ad Manager to place video ads targeted to specific demographics.
- Run interactive ads that allow viewers to engage with your content directly.
- Set budgets as low as $500 to test campaigns before scaling.
- Use geotargeting to reach local customers with pinpoint accuracy.

Instead of hoping your ad gets seen by the right people, streaming services let you ensure it does.

Billboards Reimagined: The Smart Way to Use Display Ads

Instead of spending thousands on a physical billboard that sits in one location, create a digital version and target it to the exact audience you want using display ads on Google, Facebook, and Instagram.

How to Create a Digital Billboard Ad

- Design an eye-catching billboard-style ad (use Canva or Photoshop).
- Run it as a display ad on Google, targeting users by location, interests, or search behavior.
- Use Facebook Ads Manager to place it in front of the right audience based on demographics.

- Test different creatives and optimize based on performance.

This way, instead of hoping people drive by and see your billboard, your ad follows your ideal audience wherever they go online.

The Future of Traditional Advertising Is Digital

Marketing has evolved, and so should your strategy. Podcast ads, streaming TV, and digital billboards give you the precision of digital marketing with the credibility of traditional advertising.

Why settle for mass-market guessing when you can target, track, and optimize for maximum impact?

Regardless of which marketing method you choose, always create a clear call to action (CTA). Every ad, email, or campaign must tell people exactly what to do next—call, book, buy, or sign up. Without a CTA, even the most brilliant marketing efforts will fall flat.

Before spending money on paid strategies, do your research, set clear goals, and track your results. You must know what success looks like. Are you aiming for brand awareness, lead generation, or direct sales? By keeping an eye on performance data, you can refine and optimize your marketing approach for better results.

Select marketing activities that resonate with your personality and preferences. Pick one or two ideas that align with your strengths and avoid tactics that you find daunting. If you enjoy the process, you'll stay committed, and your marketing will be more effective.

Mapping Your Marketing Strategy

- List three marketing strategies that align with your personality and business model.
- Identify one method that excites you and commit to testing it first.
- Set a small, measurable goal, such as, "Generate fifty leads from a Facebook ad campaign in thirty days."
- Outline your budget and tracking plan. What does success look like?

The only way to create CPI is to build a system that attracts leads while you focus on closing deals. Start now.

TEACH TO SELL EXERCISE

1. Select one to three strategies for lead generation that feel right for you:
   - Networking
   - Cold calling
   - Content marketing
   - Paid advertising
   - Social media outreach
2. Place these on your calendar as *non-negotiable time blocks*.
3. If using paid marketing, ensure you have an eighteen-month financial runway before implementing.
4. Track your results weekly. Adjust as needed.

CHAPTER SUMMARY: TEACH TO FIND BUSINESS

Fear is often the biggest obstacle in both life and business. We build up worst-case scenarios in our minds, but when we finally take action, we realize those fears weren't real.

In this chapter, I shared a deeply personal story about telling my daughter, Maggie, about my wife and I's decision to divorce—a conversation I had dreaded for a year. But when the moment arrived, Maggie accepted the news with love and grace. The fear that had kept me awake at night had been an illusion.

This same lesson applies to business. Many entrepreneurs hesitate to take bold action—whether it's making sales calls, marketing their services, or expanding their network—because they fear rejection or failure. But the reality is, action is always the antidote to fear.

Key Lessons

- **Fear is often an illusion.** The things we worry about the most usually turn out to be far less painful than we imagined.
- **Momentum is everything.** Just like pushing a flywheel, small daily actions in lead generation build into unstoppable success.
- **Lead generation is non-negotiable.** If you don't have enough business, nothing else matters. The top salespeople prioritize prospecting above all else.
- **Consistency beats talent.** The businesses that succeed aren't always the most talented—they're the most committed. Daily lead generation compounds into massive results.

The Flywheel Effect: How to Create No Broke Months

Success is like a heavy flywheel. At first, every push feels exhausting, and progress is slow. But as you stay consistent, momentum builds. Soon, leads start flowing effortlessly. The key is to never stop pushing; otherwise, you'll have to start from scratch.

Commit or Quit Challenge: The Choice That Defines Your Success

Every business owner reaches a moment where they must decide: take action or stay stuck in uncertainty.

Growth demands commitment. Lead generation isn't optional; it's the foundation for success. Excuses, distractions, and hesitation won't bring in clients. Consistency will.

Make a decision today. Will you dedicate yourself to daily lead generation, or will you continue making excuses?

There's no in-between. Half-commitment leads to half-results.

Set a standard for yourself. Block the time, follow through, and push past resistance. The reward? A business that thrives, opportunities that expand, and a future built on CPI.

Will you Commit or Quit?

CHAPTER 10

Teach to Convert Clients

Thirteen months after selling my brokerage, I had finally repaid my debts. I was free.

But I was still stumbling. The ashes of the brokerage held lessons that would shape my future. I realized that setbacks are only roadblocks if you let them be. My balance sheet still showed a net positive, and as long as I had more successes than failures, I was winning.

Since 2008, I had not had a single broke month. I was averaging ten sales a month and had a wealth of knowledge to share. So, during those thirteen months, I poured my heart into writing my first book, *Real Estate Evolution: The Ten-Step Guide to Consistent and Predictable Income.*

At the same time, I launched my coaching company, The **Consistent and Predictable Income Community** and www. NoBrokeMonths.com. I wasn't just selling real estate anymore; I was helping other salespeople achieve **No Broke Months** too.

But the greatest reward wasn't the financial recovery. It was the transformation.

I documented everything I had learned, and I began teaching it simply and effectively. That process of teaching restored my self-worth. Giving back, helping others—these became my mission.

And the philosophy that made it possible? *Teach to Sell.*

Teaching builds trust. It forges genuine connections. It goes beyond transactions and creates lasting relationships. When I taught, I wasn't just making sales, I was communicating value.

Through teaching, I found my worth. And so will you.

To increase your chances of being hired by clients, remember this key principle: *Teach to Sell.*

1. **Show genuine warmth and empathy.** Care for others, and they'll care for what you offer.
2. **Demonstrate knowledge confidently.** Teach effectively, and clients will trust you.
3. **Share your journey.** Let your expertise and experiences resonate with potential clients.

By integrating *Teach to Sell* into your process, you create meaningful connections that foster trust and loyalty.

Imagine a client meeting where you're not just another salesperson but a trusted advisor. Your words resonate. Your confidence shines. Your guidance feels natural. *That's the power of Teach to Sell.*

PRE-DECISION COMPASS

Before meeting a prospect, ask yourself:

- What do I know about this person beyond their immediate need?

- How can I tailor my conversation to align with their values and personality?
- What deeper motivations might be driving their decision-making?
- Am I prepared to ask meaningful questions that build trust and rapport?

PRE-DECISION TO MAKE

You can **Pre-Decide** that before every client meeting, you will take the time to research, listen, and connect.

Instead of rushing into a pitch, you will commit to understanding your prospect's mindset, tailoring your approach to their specific needs, and guiding them with trust, not pressure.

By doing this, you position yourself as a true advisor, ensuring that clients hire you not just because of what you offer, but because they trust you to lead them to the right solution.

FOCUS ON CONVERSION

Many salespeople don't struggle with lead generation. They struggle with *conversion*.

What happens when you generate leads but don't convert them?

Early in my career, I had plenty of leads but not enough conversions. I was paying staff, keeping things afloat, but barely supporting my family. Then, one day, I had no money left.

I found myself digging into my daughter's piggy bank just to afford admission to a state park for my family. That moment hit me hard. It was a wake-up call.

Failure wasn't an option. I knew if I didn't figure it out, I'd be stuck waiting tables. A lifetime of serving plates? No chance.

So, I committed. I took a hard look at what was missing and saw the problem clearly: My follow-up was weak. Success in sales isn't just about making connections; it's about staying in front of them. Conversion comes down to one thing: **consistent follow-up.**

THE SECRET TOP SALESPEOPLE KNOW

The best in the game know this: Lead generation is gold, but conversion is platinum.

Want No Broke Months? Follow up consistently.

Your next sale is probably already in your database; it's just a matter of when they'll be ready to buy. The question is: Will they choose you when the time comes?

That decision is made long before you ever meet them.

WHAT SHOULD YOU DO BEFORE MEETING A PROSPECT?

Do your homework.

Before meeting a prospect, research them online.

I once prepped for a meeting by checking a prospect's X (Twitter) feed.

The guy was an adventurer—cliff diving, hanging with tigers, exploring safaris.

Instantly, I knew:

- He's a risk-taker.
- He values speed.
- He doesn't waste time.

So, I adjusted my approach. No fluff. Straight to the point.

The meeting went like this:

Me:

"Did you receive the information I sent?"

Him:

"Yes."

Me:

"Any questions?"

Him:

"No."

Me:

"Great. Ready to get started?"

Him:

"Yes."

Me:

"Perfect. Sign here, here, and here."

He signed on the spot. Fastest deal ever.
But don't celebrate too soon.
Two days later, he fired me.
Turns out, someone who hires fast might fire fast, too.
Lesson? Know your prospect. But also, manage expectations.

HOW DO YOU CONNECT AND INFLUENCE?

Winning the deal isn't just about selling. It's about understanding.

To truly connect with a lead, you need to probe, prod, and dig deep. Unpeel the onion.

Ask powerful questions:

"Why is that important to you?"

"What does that mean for you?"

"Tell me more."

THE GOLDEN RULE OF FOLLOW-UPS

One of the first lessons I learned in sales?

Never end a conversation without setting the next step.

Every call, every meeting, end with:

"This is what happens next…"

Then, seal the next connection.

You:

"When should we next connect?"

Them:

[They give a day.]

You:

"Great! Let's lock that in. If something comes up, may I follow up the next day?"

Nine times out of ten, they'll say yes.

Then, take it further.

You:

"Fantastic! What's a good time to speak that day?"

Now, you have a firm commitment, not just a vague promise.

Master this, and you'll always stay in control of the process.

THE JOURNEY TO GET HIRED MORE OFTEN

What's the Secret to Getting Hired More Often?

A great presentation naturally leads to a prospect saying yes.

When you *Teach to Sell*, most of the work happens before you even ask for the sale.

Here's the system you can follow to increase your chances of getting hired before you even meet with a prospect.

If your sales process happens in just one step, you will need to condense these. But if your process takes multiple meetings or calls, follow each phase carefully.

What's the secret to getting
hired more often?

Step 1: The Qualification Phase

Step 2: The Fear and Bridge Concept

Step 3: The Pre-Meeting Phase

Step 4: The Getting Hired Phase

Step 1: The Qualification Phase

Speak to the Decision-Maker

Make sure you are talking to the person who can say yes. If not, schedule a time when all decision-makers are present.

Qualify Their Motivation and Ability

Do they have the need and the means to buy? If your process takes multiple steps, a short phone or video call can serve as a qualification phase.

Listen to Their Exact Words

Pay close attention to how they describe their needs. If they say:

> "I just want someone who won't mess me around."

You can later reinforce this by saying:

> "Mr. Buyer, I know you are looking for someone like me who won't mess you around. Fortunately, we met, so I can help you."

This subtle technique of embedding the words, "mess you around" help you to connect with them.

Uncover Their Pain Points

People buy for two reasons: to escape pain or move toward pleasure.

Your job is to show them how you and your service or product are the bridge from where they are to where they want to be.

Step 2: The Fear and Bridge Concept

The more pain you can identify and amplify, the easier the sale.

Why? Because people run from pain faster than they chase pleasure.

Imagine a lion charging into the room—you would bolt without thinking.

Now, imagine a treasure chest full of diamonds ten miles away. Would you sprint toward it just as fast? Probably not because you could never all-out race for that distance.

Pain makes people act instantly. Desire moves them at a steady pace.

Use this knowledge wisely.

Highlight Their Pain

Show them how your service removes it.

Make them feel the urgency to act now.

Step 3: The Pre-Meeting Phase

If your sales process has multiple steps, use this phase to Teach to Sell before the official pitch.

Send a Google Calendar Invite

Lock in the next meeting. Use language that assumes the sale:
"We look forward to helping you."
This subtly reinforces that working together is a done deal.

Send a Video Text

A simple ten-second video makes a lasting impression:

> "Mr. Buyer, it was great speaking with you.
> Just wanted to say hello so you can put a face
> to my name. I look forward to helping you."

Share Valuable Content

Send them relevant marketing materials. The more value you provide before the meeting, the easier the sale.

Agitate their pain, highlight their goals, and position yourself as the bridge.

Go all in. This is your chance to show them why you are the only logical choice.

Step 4: The Getting Hired Phase

At this point, you have done the groundwork. Now, closing the deal should feel natural.

Set Expectations

Before sealing the deal, explain what working with you will look like:

- The journey they will go on
- Common challenges that are not your fault
- The highs and lows they might experience

Why? Because setting expectations removes surprises.

Here is an example:

I once bought a car through an auction broker. It seemed like a great deal—until I got home and realized the battery was dead and the AC didn't work.

If the broker had told me upfront that auction cars often need a battery charge and a freon refill, I wouldn't have been frustrated. I would have thought,

"Ah, he's an expert. He prepared me for this."

By setting expectations, you turn potential frustrations into predictable, manageable steps.

Do the same for your prospects. Explain the highs and lows of working with you before they happen. When you do this, even if challenges arise, you remain the trusted guide, not the villain.

Seal the Deal

By this point, the sale should feel natural. But here's where you take control and guide them to a yes.

This is where *Teach to Sell* comes in.

- Share insider tips that make you look like the expert.
- Paint the picture of what it's like to work with you.
- Be honest about the challenges, and then show them how you make it easier.

    "We've helped countless people achieve results by [insert key benefit]. Imagine this: you, problem-free, cruising toward your goals with everything you need to succeed."

Then, take the lead.

    "Let's take the reins and navigate this together. You're in good hands here."

Make it clear that you are in control and they can trust you.

> "We'll tweak a few knobs, sprinkle in some
> expertise, and just like that—problem solved."

Control the pace. Keep it light yet confident.

> "So, when can we make this happen? Let's
> carve out some time and dive in."

At this moment, the decision is easy. They have seen your expertise, they trust you, and they feel like saying yes is just the next logical step.

WHAT IMPACTS HOW OFTEN YOU GET HIRED?

1. **Your skill level**—Keep improving.
2. **Your prospect's motivation and pain**—The bigger their problem (and the more you agitate it), the more they need you.

When possible, *Teach to Sell* before you even meet.

It builds trust, positions you as the expert, and makes closing effortless.

WHEN SHOULD YOU ASK FOR A REFERRAL?

The Power of the Right Timing

When I teach, I often start with a simple question:

> "When should you ask for a referral?"

The most common response I hear?

> "All the time!"

I appreciate the enthusiasm, but let's take a more strategic approach.

Asking for referrals indiscriminately can come across as desperate. Instead, there's an ideal moment to ask, a moment when your client is already primed to say "yes."

The Perfect Moment: A Thank You

The ideal time to ask for a referral is anytime your client expresses gratitude for your work.

Think about it—how do most people respond to a "Thank you"? We default to:

- "No problem."
- "It was nothing."
- "Anytime."

These responses miss an opportunity. They downplay your value and close the conversation. Instead, turn that "Thank you" into a natural gateway to a referral.

A Better Way to Respond

Next time a client thanks you, try this:

Client:

> "Thank you so much for helping me with [service or solution]."

You:

> "You're welcome! I love helping people like you.
> By the way, who do you know that also needs
> this level of care and service? Maybe someone
> in your family, workplace, or social circle?"

This approach works because the client is already in a positive emotional state, making them more likely to think of someone who could benefit from your services.

GET MORE REVIEWS—THE SILENT SALES MACHINE

I recently traveled to San Diego for a business conference. Hungry and unfamiliar with the area, I did what millions do—I pulled up Yelp.

Within seconds, I found a highly rated restaurant, read a few glowing reviews, and made my decision.

Now, think about your business.

Where Will Potential Clients Start Their Search If They Don't Have a Direct Referral?

Online.

And where will they look?

- Google
- Facebook and LinkedIn
- Your website
- Industry-specific platforms

How to Ask for a Review (The PRO Method)

Here's a simple script you can use (or teach your team to use) when asking for a review:

P—Problem or Goal

"I had a problem or a goal..."

R—Result (How you helped them)

"I found [your name or company], and they helped me by..."

O—Offer (Encouragement to contact you)

> "If you have a similar problem or goal, you
> should call [your name or company] today."

By structuring a review this way, you make it easy for clients to leave compelling, persuasive testimonials that attract more business.

Why Your Review Can Change Someone's Life

Now, let's take a step back.

Imagine an entrepreneur on the brink of giving up. A salesperson struggling to stay afloat. A business owner desperate for more clients.

Now, picture them stumbling across a review—**your review of this book**—that gives them hope.

A single review can be the difference between someone staying in business or walking away.

So, I ask for your help. Will you leave a favorable review of *Teach to Sell?*

Leaving a review takes just thirty seconds of your time, but it could make a world of difference for another entrepreneur.

Here's how you can do it:

- **Amazon**: Find the book's page and leave your positive thoughts.
- **Kindle or eReader**: Scroll down and swipe up to leave a kind review.
- **Audible**: Tap the three dots in the top-right corner, then select "Rate and Review."

Use the PRO Method for Your Review

P—Problem or Goal

> "I was struggling with (insert your specific problem or goal you had before reading this book) and needed a proven way to overcome it..."

R—Result

> "Then I discovered *Teach to Sell*, and it completely changed the way I (describe the specific breakthrough, skill, or result you achieved)..."

O—Offer

> "If you're facing the same challenge or chasing the same goal, this book is your solution—get it today!"

Your review is not just feedback, it is a beacon of encouragement for someone who needs it most.

Now, take action. **Leave a review and help another entrepreneur win.**

TEACH TO SELL EXERCISE: THE CONVERSION COMMITMENT

Conversion isn't just about closing deals; it's about leading clients through a decision-making journey where they recognize you as their trusted advisor.

In this exercise, you'll use the *Teach to Sell* method to keep your leads engaged, ensuring they don't slip through the cracks but instead become loyal, long-term clients.

To make this process even easier, download and print the accompanying worksheet. Get your free copy at www.NoBrokeMonths.com/TeachToSell and start applying this method with every client.

Step 1: Understand the "Why" Behind Every Lead

Before your next client interaction, take five minutes to analyze their true motivations. Fill in the answers below to sharpen your understanding of their needs:

What challenge or pain point is this client trying to solve?
Example: They are frustrated with their current service provider, unsure about the process, or feeling overwhelmed.

____

____

____

What fears, hesitations, or objections might be holding them back?
Example: Uncertainty about cost, fear of making the wrong choice, lack of trust in salespeople.

____

____

____

What deeper emotional drivers influence their decision?
Example: Security, freedom, recognition, certainty, success, status.

____

____

____

____

Clients don't buy because of facts; they buy because of emotions. The more you understand **why they need a solution**, the easier it becomes to guide them toward a confident decision.

Step 2: Teach to Build Trust, Not Just Sell

Instead of rushing into a pitch, focus on educating and empowering your client by using the three strategies below. Write out how you can apply them in your next conversation.

Share valuable insights: Provide an industry trend, strategy, or perspective they might not know.

What insights could you share?

____

____

____

____

Break down the process: Give them clarity on how things work so they feel in control.

How does the process work?

____

____

____

____

Tell a transformation story: Share a real example of how a past client overcame a similar challenge.

For example, if a lead is hesitant to commit, you could say:

> "I completely understand. Many of my clients felt the same way at first.

> "One of them, [client name], wasn't sure if now was the right time to move forward.

> "But once we went through the numbers and they saw the long-term impact, they realized waiting would cost them more in the end. Now, they're grateful they made the decision. Here's how it played out for them..."

Write your story:

____

____

____

____

By teaching rather than pressuring, you create trust and position yourself as the logical choice.

Step 3: Lock in the Next Step Before Ending the Conversation

The biggest mistake salespeople make? Leaving conversations open-ended.

Before wrapping up, always establish the next commitment from the prospect.

Ask this question:

"What would you need to see or know to feel completely confident moving forward?"

____

____

____

Reinforce the logical next step:

"Based on everything we've discussed, the best next step is [insert action]. Let's go ahead and schedule that now so we can keep the momentum going."

What will be your specific next step with this prospect?

____

____

____

This removes uncertainty and ensures the deal doesn't stall.

ACTION CHALLENGE: APPLY THIS TODAY

At each sales encounter, follow this three-step process:

1. Uncover the client's true motivations before the meeting.
2. Teach them something valuable during the conversation.
3. End with a firm next step to keep the deal moving forward.

After each interaction, reflect on your results.

Did the conversation flow more naturally?

____

____

____

Did the client seem more engaged?

____

____

____

Were they more confident in their decision?

____

____

____

Mastering *Teach to Sell* isn't just about improving your conversion rate—it's about becoming the type of professional clients trust, respect, and refer to others.

CHAPTER SUMMARY: TEACH TO CONVERT CLIENTS

Success isn't just about making sales; it's about teaching your prospects why they should choose you before you even ask for the sale. That's the power of *Teach to Sell*.

After selling my brokerage and paying off my debts, I realized that my true breakthrough wasn't just in financial recovery—it was in transformation.

By documenting my journey, and launching the CPI Community, I discovered that teaching built trust, positioned me as an authority, and led to deeper, more meaningful client relationships.

Key Takeaways

- *Teach to Sell* **builds trust.** When you teach, you're not just selling; you're positioning yourself as the go-to expert.
- **Conversion is more important than lead generation.** Leads mean nothing without follow-up. The best salespeople focus on consistent, strategic follow-ups.
- **Understand your prospect.** Research their needs, motivations, and pain points before every meeting.
- **Use the follow-up formula.** Never leave a conversation without setting the next step.
- **Set expectations early.** Clients who understand the process upfront are less likely to back out later.
- **Ask for referrals at the right moment.** The best time to ask is when a client expresses gratitude.

This chapter gives you a clear system to increase your chances of getting hired before you even meet with a prospect. If you apply these principles, you'll transform the way clients see you, and you'll win more business as a result.

Commit or Quit Challenge: Your Resurrection Moment

Every hero's journey has a moment of truth, a test that demands everything from them. This is where the weak give up, and the strong rise.

This is *your* moment.

You've worked hard. You've built momentum. But something is missing. The conversions aren't coming fast enough. The follow-ups feel inconsistent. You know you could be closing more deals, yet something is holding you back.

This is your test.

You can let doubt creep in. You can make excuses. Or you can rise.

I've been where you are. My own test came when I realized I wasn't converting at the level I needed. Leads were coming in, but I wasn't closing them. My business was on the line. I hit rock bottom, borrowing money from my daughter's piggy bank just to get by.

I committed. I mastered conversion. I transformed my business. And now, I'm handing you the same challenge.

Your Challenge: Over the next seven days, track every lead you interact with. Before each meeting or call, research your prospect. Find one key insight about them and tailor your approach accordingly.

Will you Commit or Quit?

Part III

BUILD AN ORGANIZATION

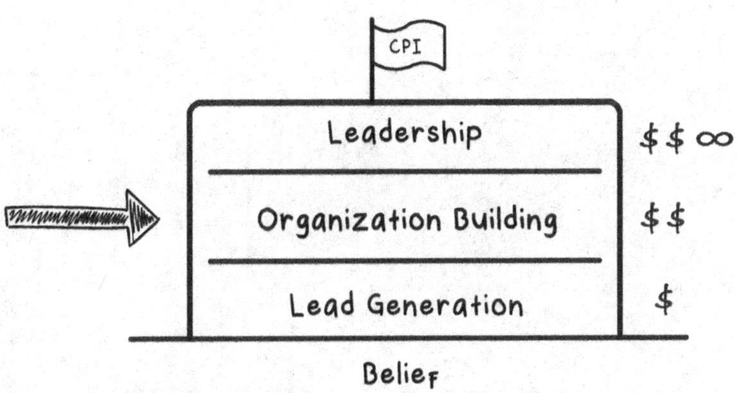

CHAPTER 11

Teach to Hire the Right People

FACING THE FEAR OF UNWORTHINESS

Imagine yourself standing in the shadows of your past, facing the most profound fear that has always haunted you: the gnawing sense of being unworthy.

Memories—perhaps of abandonment, loneliness, and painful experiences—flood your mind. Each one flashes before you like scenes from a painful movie, making your heart pound and your hands tremble.

A relentless chant echoes in your mind: *I'm not good enough. I'm not smart enough.*

But this time, you stand tall.

You take a deep breath and close your eyes. In the darkness, you see the faces of those who believed in you—a teacher who showed you kindness, a friend who guided you through struggle, and a loved one who saw your worth.

As you open your eyes, the shadow of unworthiness stands before you. It mutters old beliefs, trying to drag you back into the abyss.

But you are different now.

You step forward, your heart filled with determination, and confront the shadow with the truth of your journey.

You declare with a strong and unwavering voice:

"I am worthy!"

The shadow wavers, flickering like a dying flame.

"I am worthy of love, success, and happiness. I have faced my fears, conquered my demons, and risen above my past. I have built trust, helped others, and made a difference.

"My past does not define my worth—my actions and the love I give do."

The shadow shrinks, retreating before the light of your truth. The doubts and fears that once held you captive lose their power. You are no longer the scared, unworthy child. You are a warrior who has fought and won the greatest battle of all—the struggle within.

Now, it's time for the next challenge: building a team that will help you achieve your vision.

WHAT DO YOU NEED TO KNOW ABOUT LEADERSHIP?

Just as you confronted your fears and transformed your mindset, stepping into leadership requires the same courage.

Before I explain how to build an organization, let's pause briefly to touch upon leadership, because who you become as a leader will determine who you attract.

Understanding how you lead is crucial before you start hiring. Your leadership style will dictate who joins your team and whether they will thrive within your vision.

HIRING TO BUILD AN ORGANIZATION

To effectively build an organization, leadership is key. Your ability to hire the right people depends on your ability to lead.

A great leader asks:

- Would you hire someone like you?
- Would you want to work for someone like you?

Your mission as a leader should be helping others get what they want. When you do this well, your own success becomes inevitable.

As you refine your leadership skills, consider these three crucial questions:

1. What do I think?
2. Who do I know?
3. What words will I choose?

Leadership is about clarity of vision, guiding others toward success, and creating an environment that attracts and retains top talent.

PRE-DECISION COMPASS: ALIGNING YOUR LEADERSHIP WITH YOUR HIRING STRATEGY

Before you begin hiring, reflect on your own experiences with leadership and teamwork.

Ask yourself:

- Have I ever worked under a leader who inspired me? What qualities did they have?
- Have I ever worked for a leader who drained my motivation? What qualities did they lack?
- What kind of leader do I aspire to be?
- How will I ensure that I attract the right people to my vision?

PRE-DECISION TO MAKE

Before you hire, decide that you will not settle for mediocrity. Commit to attracting, developing, and retaining high-caliber individuals who align with your vision and values.

TEACH TO SELL: FROM HIRING TO BUILDING A LEGACY

When I started in sales, my first question was simple:

"How can I get more business?"

As my business matured, I realized that opportunities were abundant. The more important question became:

"How can I attract the right people to work
for me?"

This shift in mindset changed everything. Success in business isn't just about making sales; it's about building the right team to create something bigger than yourself.

The best hires weren't just looking for a job; **they aspired to attain my position and were willing to do whatever it took to support my advancement.**

This led me to an even bigger question:

"How can I replicate my abilities in others?
Who should I partner with for mutual success?"

I recognized that true success wasn't about doing everything myself—it hinged on investing in others.

That meant:

- Setting a vision
- Equipping my team with the right tools
- Establishing clear expectations
- Removing obstacles
- Stepping aside to let them thrive

Teaching, training, adding value, and fostering accountability became my **most valuable leadership strategies**.

TEACH TO SELL IN HIRING: ASKING THE RIGHT QUESTIONS

My coaches challenged me to expand my vision, to make it bigger. They pushed me to build a twenty-year plan and ask myself:

- How do I create a business that transforms lives and leaves a lasting impact?
- What am I doing to foster an environment that attracts elite leaders?
- Who can partner with me?
- Who do I need to become to lead a team of leaders, each earning $1 million a year while helping others achieve their highest potential?

I identified a half dozen leaders and vowed to model their success. Now, it's your turn.

THE TRUTH ABOUT HIRING: WHY IT'S NOT JUST ABOUT FINDING THE RIGHT PEOPLE

> *Years go by fast. So, I choose not to spend them acting small.*
>
> *I understand that to impact people's lives in a massive way and for me to live the most meaningful life possible that I will have to succeed through others.*
>
> —Dan Rochon
>   (*notes from my journal*)

Over the years, I've built an incredible team. People often ask me about my hiring secret.

The truth? I don't have one.

Despite following a structured process, I only get hiring right about 50 percent of the time.

But where I excel is in retaining the right individuals. I consider myself a *collector of talent*.

Now, why should you take hiring advice from someone who gets it wrong half the time?

Because without a structured process, you're likely to fail over 90 percent of the time, and because understanding how to retain top talent is just as important—if not more—than hiring them in the first place.

Hiring isn't just about filling roles; it's about building a leadership-driven business that attracts, develops, and retains top talent. That's how you

Teach to Sell, not just in business, but in building a legacy.

SET THE VISION: INSPIRE, ALIGN, AND ATTRACT THE RIGHT PEOPLE

Before you can hire the right people, you need to know where you're going. This is called your vision.

Great leaders don't just hire employees, they recruit believers in a bigger mission. Your vision is the foundation that attracts, aligns, and retains the best talent.

WHY VISION MATTERS IN HIRING

Influential leaders define their vision, communicate it often, and bring people into alignment with it. Your vision is the North Star that guides every hiring decision and ensures that you're building a team that is passionate, driven, and invested in the same mission.

The best people don't just want a paycheck, they want to be part of something bigger than themselves. Your vision should be that bigger thing.

THE POWER OF A BIG VISION

Your vision must be so big, so compelling, that when someone joins your organization, they see it as a vehicle to achieve their own highest aspirations.

A bold vision attracts A-players—people who want to be part of something transformative. These individuals will not only work for you but work with you to drive the mission forward.

MAKE YOUR VISION CLEAR, BIG, AND CONSTANT

To attract **top talent**, your vision must be:

- **Crystal clear.** If your team can't explain your vision in one sentence, it's too vague.
- **Expansive.** A vision that only serves you is too small. Make it about others.
- **Repeated often.** The best leaders talk about their vision **constantly**.

Jack Welch, one of the most successful CEOs of modern times, understood this better than anyone.

> Good business leaders create a vision, artic-
> ulate the vision, passionately own the vision,
> and relentlessly drive it to completion.
>
> Above all else, good leaders are open.
>
> They go up, down, and around their organiza-
> tion to reach people. They do not stick to the
> established channels. They are informal. They
> are straight with people. They make a religion
> out of being accessible. They never get bored
> telling their story. (Welch & Byrne, 2001)

During Welch's tenure at General Electric, the company's value rose by more than 4,000 percent—proof that a well-communicated vision isn't just inspiring; it's profitable.

YOUR NEXT STEP

1. **Write down your vision.** Can you clearly state where your business is going in one sentence?
2. **Communicate it constantly**. Say it so often that your team can repeat it verbatim.

3. **Hire for vision alignment**. When interviewing candidates, ask:

   a) "What excites you about this vision?"

   b) "How do you see yourself contributing to it?"

   c) "Where do you want to be in five years, and how does this vision align with that?"

People don't just want a job. They want a mission to believe in.

If your vision is powerful enough, the right people will see joining your team as a no-brainer.

Consider a world where no salesperson ever experiences a broke month again, where your success isn't left to chance, market conditions, or sheer hustle, but built on a proven, repeatable system that guarantees results.

That's the vision of the CPI Community—a movement designed to put an end to financial uncertainty and give sales professionals the tools, strategies, and support to create income they can count on, month after month.

If this speaks to you, if you're ready to take control of your business, your income, and your future, hit me up. Let's build your success story together.

SHAPING CULTURE: THE FOUNDATION OF A THRIVING TEAM

Building a Winning Team: Who Belongs in Your Culture?

Your company's success is directly tied to the people you surround yourself with.

Before you hire, ask yourself:

- Who do I need on my team to bring my vision to life?
- Do my current team members align with my values?
- Am I attracting people who elevate the culture or drain it?

The best teams are built with intentionality, not just filling positions, but selecting individuals who align with your mission.

The Type of People to Look For

You need team members who are driven, growth-oriented, and committed to success. They should thrive in an environment where learning, accountability, and results matter.

Patrick Lencioni, author of *The Five Dysfunctions of a Team*, emphasizes that great team members are:

- **Coachable.** They are open to feedback and eager to improve.
- **Willing.** They step up when needed and take ownership.
- **Hungry.** They have a deep drive for success (I prefer they're starving!).

To make it easy to spot top talent, I use an acronym: **SCARLeT.**

SCARLeT: The Behaviors of Top Performers

- **Self-starter**—Do they take initiative, solve problems, and own their results?
- **Competitive**—Do they have a drive to win and push for excellence?
- **Assertive**—Are they confident in making decisions and taking action?
- **Relationship-based**—Do they thrive on collaboration and build strong connections?
- **Learning-based**—Are they naturally curious and eager to grow?

- **Team player**—Do they prioritize team success over individual recognition?

Hiring with SCARLeT in Mind

During the hiring process, evaluate candidates against these six traits to determine if they are a culture fit or a red flag.

Here's what to look for:

Self-Starters
- Do they take ownership of problems, or do they wait to be told what to do?
- Do they bring solutions instead of excuses?

Competitive
- Do they set high goals for themselves and push to exceed them?
- Do they see challenges as obstacles or opportunities?

Assertive
- Can they confidently share ideas and make decisions?
- Do they take action even when they're uncertain?

Relationship-based
- Do they genuinely enjoy working with others?
- Are they energized by teamwork or drained by it?

Learning-based
- Are they naturally curious and adaptable?
- Do they seek out new skills and knowledge on their own?

Team players
- Do they celebrate team wins as much as individual achievements?

- Are they willing to collaborate, support, and uplift those around them?

The Bottom Line: Culture Starts with You

If you want a strong culture, it starts with the standards you set and the people you bring in.

- **Define your values** so you attract the right people.
- **Hire for SCARLeT traits** so your team is aligned and motivated.
- **Lead by example** because culture reflects leadership.

A winning team isn't built by accident—it's designed with purpose. The question is, are you ready to build yours?

FROM CULTURE TO MISSION: THE NEXT STEP IN BUILDING A HIGH-PERFORMING TEAM

You've defined your culture, your values, and the type of people who belong in your organization. Now, it's time to bring it all together by crafting a mission—your company's guiding purpose that aligns your vision with your people.

Your mission is not just a statement on a wall, it's the driving force behind every decision you make, from hiring to leadership to daily operations. It gives meaning to the work you do and inspires people to commit to something bigger than a paycheck.

The key to *Teach to Sell* is simple: People don't buy products or services, they buy into a mission that resonates with them. The same applies to hiring. If you want to attract the right people, your mission must be so compelling that they see working with you as the only logical choice.

WHAT IS A MISSION?

A mission is the goal of your company, the map that leads you from where you are today to where you want to be.

Once you've defined your vision, ask yourself two critical questions:

1. How will I get there?
2. Who will help me get there?

Your business doesn't grow because you wish it would; it grows because you build the right team to execute your mission. But to do that, you must first understand what drives them.

YOUR MISSION MUST ALIGN WITH YOUR PEOPLE'S GOALS

One of the biggest mistakes leaders make is expecting people to blindly follow their mission without considering their personal goals. That's not leadership; it's dictatorship.

To build a team that is fully invested in your vision, you must first invest in them. When you align your company's mission with the personal goals of your team members, you create a win-win environment where everyone thrives.

Want to inspire people to work with you? Help them achieve their own dreams while working toward yours.

FIND AND HIRE THE RIGHT TALENT: THE WHO OVER THE WHAT

Now that you've established your Vision, Culture, Values, People, and Mission, it's time to hire.

Here's the truth:

The difference between where you are and where you want to be is not in the "what." It's in the "who."

When you shift your focus from "What do I need to do" to "Who do I need to hire," your growth becomes exponential instead of incremental.

The right people own the outcome. They don't just fill a role—they drive the mission forward.

But how do you find them?

HOW TO HIRE PEOPLE WHO OWN THE OUTCOME

The key to hiring the right people is predictability. You need a proven process that ensures your hires align with your mission, culture, and expectations.

Here's what you must do:

- **Set clear expectations from the start.** People perform best when they know exactly what is expected of them.
- **Look for 100 percent commitment.** Skills can be developed, but drive and dedication must already exist.
- **Observe their actions, not just their words.** A resume doesn't tell the whole story. Watch how they show up, how they handle challenges, and how they take initiative.
- **Make sure they choose to commit or quit.** People should make a conscious decision to go all-in or walk away. You don't want people who "try" the job; you want people who own the mission.

ALWAYS LOOK FOR TALENTED PEOPLE

- The best hires aren't found when you're desperate to fill a role. They're cultivated long before you need them.

If you want to build an elite team, you must always be recruiting.

But attracting top talent isn't about having the best offer, it's about having proof of concept. The people you want to hire will ask:

- What value do you provide?
- How is your business different from everyone else?
- How will working with you change my life?

If you can answer these questions with clarity and conviction, you'll never struggle to attract top talent.

To grow, you will want to attract high-ability people.

DO GREAT SALESPEOPLE MAKE GREAT BUSINESS OWNERS?

The ability to sell and the ability to lead are two different skill sets.

As a salesperson, you're great at:

- Building relationships
- Making quick decisions
- Influencing people

But those same strengths can work against you when it comes to hiring.

Why? Because great salespeople often "sell" bad hires into the role instead of selecting the right fit. You don't want to "win" a bad hire just because they're interviewing with your competitor— you want to find the best person for the job.

TEACH TO SELL INSIGHT

Hiring is not about persuading someone to join your team. It's about creating an opportunity so compelling that the right people feel like they can't afford to miss it.

THE HIGH COST OF A BAD HIRE

Hiring the wrong person doesn't just slow you down; it can cost you exponentially more than you think.

The consequences of a bad hire include:

- Financial loss
- Decreased team morale
- Extra workload for other employees
- Stress and frustration
- Damage to your company culture
- Lost credibility with clients

HAVE I MADE BAD HIRES?

Absolutely.

I've hired:

- A salesperson who showed up to meetings intoxicated
- Someone who was found in the office at 10 p.m. in their underwear
- A CFO who embezzled over $100,000 from my company

Yes, these things really happened. And they cost me more than just money. They impacted my business, my team, and my family.

The worst part? The signs were there. I just didn't know how to recognize them at the time.

That's why I now follow a proven process to hire and retain the right people—and why you should, too.

BALANCING HIRING AND SELLING: WHY BOTH MATTER FOR GROWTH

Most business owners make a critical mistake; they focus only on lead generation while ignoring talent acquisition.

They think, *If I just get more clients, my business will grow.* But that's a short-sighted approach.

Because here's the truth: Your business will only grow as fast as the people you bring into it.

If you're constantly chasing sales but not investing in building the right team, you're setting yourself up for burnout and bottlenecks.

THE 50/50 RULE: HIRING AND SELLING GO HAND IN HAND

To prevent bad hires and scale effectively, you must commit to spending 50 percent of your lead generation time identifying and recruiting top talent.

Imagine how different your business could look if, instead of always focusing on clients, you also focused on attracting and developing the best people to help you serve those clients.

Because here's what most people don't realize: Finding the right person is easier than making the wrong person great.

That's why you must be as strategic about hiring as you are about sales.

HIRING LIKE A SPECIAL FORCES TEAM: ONLY THE BEST MAKE IT

Think of elite sales teams like top military units.

The goal isn't to compare business to warfare, it's to highlight that excellence requires an elite selection process.

Take the Navy SEALs, for example. Only 6 percent of applicants even meet the requirements to start training, and only one in four who start will actually finish. That means for every sixty-five men who apply, only one becomes a SEAL. (Couch, 2003)

Why does this matter?

Because if you want to lead a top-tier team, you must be willing to weed through many people who won't make the cut.

That means:

- Building relationships with a deep pool of potential candidates before you need them
- Recognizing that not everyone is a fit, and that's okay
- Setting the bar high and only hiring those who match your vision, culture, and values

WANT TO BE THE BEST? BUILD A BENCH OF TOP TALENT

If you want to be the best in your field, you can't do it alone.

The most successful businesses aren't built on one person working harder. They're built on leaders who attract, develop, and empower other leaders.

Hiring isn't just about filling roles, it's about building a system that continually produces top performers. That's why hiring isn't a one-time task. It's a strategic growth lever that separates struggling businesses from industry leaders.

But here's where most leaders get stuck: They wait until they "need" someone before looking for talent. By then, it's too late.

WHY YOU NEED A TALENT BENCH

In business, just like in sports, your team is only as strong as its depth chart.

In the NFL, teams inevitably lose key players throughout the season. The successful ones, however, boast a robust bench—a roster of skilled backups ready to step in at any moment.

If you don't actively build a talent bench, you're at the mercy of your first hires.

Think about it: What happens if a key employee quits or underperforms?

If you don't have a strong replacement ready, your business suffers.

The best leaders don't wait for talent gaps to appear. They prepare for them in advance.

HOW TO BUILD A TALENT PIPELINE LIKE AN NFL GENERAL MANAGER

NFL teams don't just focus on their starting lineup; they plan for every scenario.

Backup players are trained and developed in case the starters go down.

Practice squad players train with the team, so if a roster spot opens, they can step in.

Scouts are always tracking potential recruits, ensuring they can pick up the right talent when the time comes.

This intentional depth is why elite teams stay competitive even when challenges arise.

The same principle applies to your business.

Your backup quarterback should be talented enough to be a starter on another team because one day, they might end up being yours.

HOW TO APPLY THIS TO YOUR BUSINESS USING *TEACH TO SELL*

A great sales pitch isn't about persuading someone to buy today; it's about planting the seed so that when the time is right, they already know they want in.

The same goes for hiring. You shouldn't just recruit when you need someone. You should always be engaging, nurturing, and attracting top talent.

Here's how:

- **Always be scouting.** Keep tabs on talented professionals before you need them.
- **Have a "practice squad."** Stay in touch with people who aren't the right fit today but could be tomorrow.
- **Think long-term.** Build relationships with high performers so that when a position opens, the best people already want to work with you.

THE BUSINESS LESSON: STAY AHEAD OF THE GAME

If you wait until a star player gets injured to find a replacement, it's already too late.

The same applies to business. If you don't have a talent bench, you'll always be playing from behind.

Build your team before you need it. That way, when an opportunity—or a challenge—arises, you'll already have the right people in place.

The question isn't whether you need a bench. The question is, how strong is yours?

KNOW THE TRAITS OF SUCCESS

Should you ever hire someone you are less than 100 percent sure will succeed?

When hiring, if it is not a "Hell, yes!" it is a no.

What do you do if you do not believe the candidate will succeed at any point in the interview?

If you have a concern at the end of any step of the interview process, stop the interview and exit it with class.

There are no "yellow lights" at the end of each level.

If it is not a bright, "green light," then it is a "red light." Leave the interview gracefully.

How do you part ways if you are not a good match?

When you are interviewing to hire and discover it is not a good fit, end the conversation so that you honor the person you are interviewing and leave them empowered.

Tell them that it is your responsibility to match the proper role to the right person and that you will be doing them a disservice to place them in the position you are hiring.

If you have another role that might fit the candidate, transition the conversation to that opportunity. If you have no position that suits them, do your best to help them find another option with another company.

TEACH TO SELL EXERCISES

Exercise 1: Define Your Vision for Growth

Ask yourself:

- What do I see my company achieving?

____

____

____

- How can I communicate this vision clearly to those I lead?

____

____

____

- How often do I reinforce my vision with my team?

____

____

____

Write down your responses. If you struggle to articulate your vision in one sentence, refine it until it's crystal clear.

Exercise 2: Identify Your Core Values

If you're unsure of your core values, ask yourself:

- Who do I admire most in my life?

____

____

____

- What qualities do they have that I respect?

____

____

____

- What values have guided me in my most important decisions?

Here are some common core values to help spark ideas:

  - Integrity
  - Achievement
  - Creativity
  - Courage
  - Growth
  - Leadership
  - Impact

____

____

____

List your top three values and how they shape your hiring decisions.

____

____

____

____

Exercise 3: Attracting the Right People

Hiring isn't just about finding the right person; it's about being the kind of leader that top talent wants to follow.

Ask yourself:

- Would I want to work for someone like me?

____

____

____

____

- Would I hire myself for this role?

____

____

____

____

- What can I improve to attract the best people?

____

____

____

____

- Write down three actions you can take to become the kind of leader that naturally attracts top talent.

____

____

____

Exercise 4: Building a Talent Bench

Answer the following:

- Do I have a list of people I'd like to recruit when the opportunity arises?

____

____

____

- How can I start conversations with high performers before I need them?

____

____

____

- What is my plan for developing and retaining top talent?

____

____

____

Commit to reaching out to at least one potential future hire this week and building a relationship with them.

CHAPTER SUMMARY: TEACH TO HIRE THE RIGHT PEOPLE

- **Leadership defines hiring.** Before you hire, define who you are as a leader because you will attract people who reflect your leadership style.
- **Your vision attracts the right talent.** People don't just want a job; they want a mission to believe in. The clearer and bigger your vision, the more top performers will want to join you.
- **Culture is created, not discovered.** The way your team operates is a direct reflection of the standards you set and uphold.
- **Hiring is a process, not an event.** The right hires own the outcome and align with your vision, culture, and values.
- **Building a talent bench is crucial.** The best organizations prepare for talent gaps before they happen by always recruiting, training, and nurturing future hires.
- **You must split your time between hiring and selling.** Growth requires both client acquisition and talent acquisition. Neglecting either will limit your success.

- **The cost of a bad hire is high.** A poor hiring decision can damage morale, decrease productivity, and cost you financially—this is why a structured hiring process is non-negotiable.

The most successful leaders don't just fill positions—they build teams that drive their vision forward. Are you ready to hire with purpose?

Commit or Quit Challenge: Own Your Leadership and Hiring Strategy

At the start of this chapter, you may have questioned your ability to lead, attract top talent, and build a team that will move your business forward. Now, the choice is yours:

You can either:

1. **Commit** to hiring with intention, developing strong leadership skills, and surrounding yourself with the best people to scale your business.
2. **Quit** by staying stuck in the cycle of doing everything yourself, delaying decisions, and hoping things improve on their own.

Your challenge:

- Write down three specific actions you will take to strengthen your leadership and hiring process.
- Take one of those actions within the next twenty-four hours.
- Hold yourself accountable. Your success depends on the people you choose to work with.

If you don't intentionally build your team, your business will remain limited by what you can accomplish alone. The best leaders don't just attract the right people; they create an environment where top talent wants to stay, grow, and succeed.

Are you ready to own your leadership and hiring strategy, or will you continue waiting for the "right time" that never comes? The choice is yours.

Will you Commit or Quit?

Part IV

LEAD YOUR PEOPLE

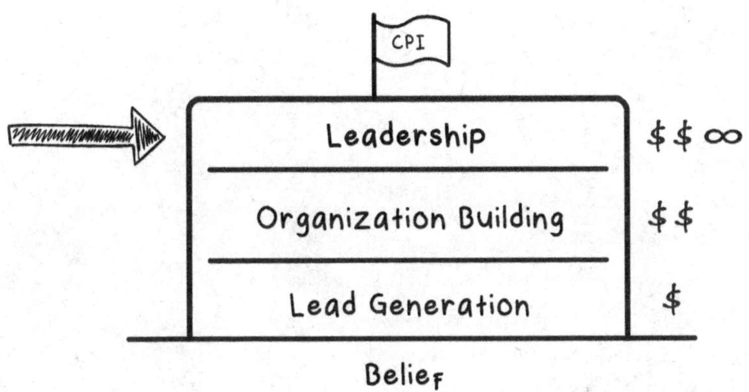

CHAPTER 12

Teach to Helps Others Get What They Want

Owning a brokerage was an incredible journey of growth, leadership, and impact. However, the next chapter of my career challenged me to lead in a new way.

When I transitioned from brokerage owner to agent within the franchise, I had the opportunity to refine my leadership skills in ways I hadn't before.

Rather than managing a large operation, I shifted my focus to direct mentorship, coaching, and guiding individuals toward their highest potential.

I found new ways to lift others, not just by structuring systems but by empowering them to think, make decisions, and take ownership of their success.

This shift deepened my commitment to creating an impact, one conversation and one relationship at a time.

Leadership had never been about authority for me; it had always been about service and influence. But this transition heightened my awareness of what truly matters in leadership: helping people recognize and achieve their potential.

I embraced effective communication, holding daily power-up sessions that fostered accountability, collaboration, and trust.

These weren't just check-ins; they were opportunities for people to step up, contribute ideas, and take action. Leadership wasn't just about delegation, it was about investment in others.

One team member, known for her exceptional organizational skills, rose to lead operations and eventually launched two companies of her own.

Another, initially uncertain in negotiations, developed confidence through coaching and went on to close high-profile deals. A third, hesitant about stepping into leadership, gained confidence through structured mentorship and now leads a thriving division.

By leading with integrity and empathy, we achieved remarkable outcomes—surpassing sales targets, earning industry recognition, and creating a culture of success that extended far beyond business.

PRE-DECISION COMPASS: EMBRACING LEADERSHIP GROWTH

Reflect on your past experiences where you had to lead or guide others. What challenges did you face, and how did you overcome them? Leadership is a skill that is developed over time through conscious effort and learning.

Ask yourself:

- When have I taken on a leadership role, even when it wasn't official?
- What leadership qualities do I naturally possess, and which ones do I need to develop?
- How has my approach to leadership changed based on past experiences?
- What would happen if I fully embraced my ability to lead with confidence?

PRE-DECISION TO MAKE

You can **Pre-Decide** that when challenges arise in your leadership journey, you will embrace them as growth opportunities.

Instead of doubting your ability, you will remind yourself that leadership is about continuous learning, adapting, and guiding others toward success.

UNDERSTAND PURPOSEFUL LEADERSHIP

> Purposeful Leadership = Intentional Awareness

The Spectrum of Leadership: Good vs. Bad Leaders

Leadership takes many forms, but not all leaders create positive results. Leadership, at its core, is about influence, and influence can be used for good or bad.

I once asked colleagues who they considered the worst leaders of all time. The responses included cult figures, tyrannical rulers, and corporate fraudsters. These individuals had the ability to lead, but their influence was destructive.

The lesson? Leadership itself is neutral. It's how you lead that determines your impact. This is why it's critical to vet those you follow and commit to being the best leader you can be for those who choose to follow you.

Traits of an Effective Leader

I've gained valuable insights from mentors and experience, and the most impactful leaders exhibit these traits:

- **Inter-dependent**—They think for themselves while guiding others.
- **Problem solver**—They don't dwell on obstacles; they find solutions.
- **Consistent**—They lead by example, maintaining stability and reliability.
- **Big vision**—They see beyond the present and guide others toward a bigger future.
- **Action-oriented**—They cause people to do more, inspiring action rather than passive compliance.

How to Become a Purposeful Leader

A purposeful leader does not meet people in the middle. Instead, they meet people where they are and guide them toward where they want to go.

This requires applying the *Teach to Sell* approach—helping people think differently so they can achieve what they truly desire.

What a Purposeful Leader Must Do

A purposeful leader's primary responsibility is to teach others how to think so they can get what they want.

This means:

- Understanding that leadership is a responsibility, not a title
- Sharing clear instruction while fostering independent decision-making
- Developing self-awareness and emotional intelligence to lead with authenticity
- Helping others overcome limiting beliefs by guiding them through *Teach to Sell* principles

Lead Others

In sales, you often show your clients the way.

Sometimes, you will lead the client.

Other times you will persuade other vendors.

If you have a team, you will lead them.

What if you believe you are not a leader?

Everybody leads another in some manner. For example, you might direct your spouse, and they will guide you in other instances. Likewise, you might lead a child or a friend.

How does your leadership extend from your direct interactions?

The nature of influence allows for a ripple effect. You can impact people whom you have never met through the way you lead those who are close to you.

Will increasing your leadership make your business better?
To build a great business, focus on growing your people and creating a great company.

What is best for others you lead to know?
The team should believe that what they do is important and has meaning. People need to have clarity about what they are supposed to do and be able to depend on each other. They should feel safe expressing their concerns and thoughts.

Have the right people in the right roles performing at the right level.
The people you lead have more impact on the outcome than you.

When leading, do you ask others to meet you where you are?
As a leader, your job is not to meet people in the middle. It is to meet people where they are and then help take them where they want to go.

Come from providing value to people so they can receive the most out of life.

What do you do when there are problems?
When problems arise, offer a solution by pointing out how to fix the problem in a way that will best help the individual you lead. You will need a different approach for each individual or team to be the most effective.

What do you do if you have critical feedback for another person?
If you must mention critical feedback, remember that a barber lathers a man before he shaves him.

Seek first to find positive input and then share vital and specific strategies they could implement to improve.

Give care, then candor.
When stressful situations occur, be sensitive and present. Provide praise in public and critical recommendations in private. Remember that the intention is to help.

What is the path you will learn leadership in sales?
At the beginning of your sales career, the only resource that you have is yourself.

Then you hire one or two people, and you do the business together. When you develop your ability to lead others so they may get what they want, then they will lead your business, and you will grow exponentially.

ABOUT WORKING TOGETHER

Does working together make you a team?
Being a part of a group does not make you a team.

When you form a group, the result is often a setback. However, when that group becomes a team, the propulsion can be exponential.

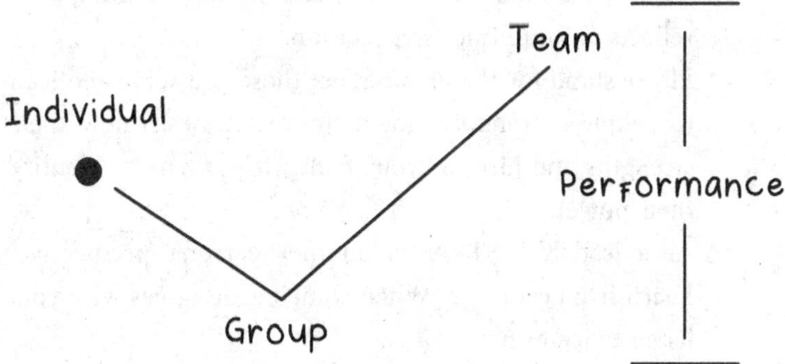

Your success is mutual with those you lead.
It would help if you engineered the team to succeed at an optimal level, with each member taking on their duties entirely. You are responsible for understanding that your actions impact others.

Does your success only depend on those you lead directly?
This practice applies to your extended team, including lenders, title companies, home inspectors, and so on. Together, you will achieve more. Insist that your organization uses your preferred vendors when they can.

TIPS AND TRICKS TO LEAD BETTER

What have I learned about leadership in sales?
Throughout the years, I have discovered more lessons than I could have believed. As a result, I have experienced "messy" in the past as well as success.

What are some of the most valuable lessons I have learned while building a team?

- Set expectations for your relationships. A complaint reflects an unfulfilled expectation.
- Please stand for the greatness of those you serve and lead to people's strengths, not their weaknesses. Know their strengths and hire for your fault. Help others to identify their power.
- As a leader, LISTEN to another person's perspective. Learn from criticism. When someone disagrees with you, listen twice as hard.

Always ask,

"What can I do differently?"

Always strive to hear.
Consider all opinions and then select an option of direction based on what is best for the whole group or team. Finally, examine what will allow us to reach our goal more quickly.

- Respond instead of reacting. When a problem arises, think about the best solutions before you act.

A well-thought-out response will allow for success than a quick reaction.

- Every problem has a solution, and it will be best to face challenges head-on.
- Move obstacles out of the way. Move the constraints.
- As a leader, do not interrupt a team member when they speak. You can best demonstrate that you are listening by being quiet and then restating what someone says after they say it. Always be sure that all speak before a meeting concludes.

How do you remove the restrictions?
- Teams succeed when everyone feels they can speak up and have a voice.
- Create opportunities for others.
- Understand that your job is to lead so that others can think and act as they desire to reach their goals.
- Attract people who believe in themselves and act. I noticed that those who thrive possess competitiveness, like to learn, are assertive, relate to others, are team players, and are self-starters.
- Be 100 percent accountable and authentic to your responsibility for the results. Measure results, not effort. Strive to obtain incremental gains.

- As a sales leader, your job is to find business, find talented people with unlimited thinking, and train, lead, and develop them.
- As a leader, when there is a failure, look in the mirror. When there is a success, search through a window.
- You never get paid to be correct. Instead, you get paid to persuade.
- Foster a culture of continuous learning and growth. Encourage ongoing development through training programs, mentorship opportunities, and a commitment to personal and professional advancement for every team member.

Is it essential to always be "right"?
Holding on to being right will create a barrier and keep you from listening.

Can you be effective by always placing your people first?
Leading while serving does not mean you must negate the conviction of your beliefs. On the contrary, when you are more committed to achieving the outcome than being right, you will better understand.

What poisons a team?
1. Gossip
2. Incompetence
3. Lack of unity
4. Personal ambitions that outweigh those of the team
5. Missing cohesion

RETAIN TALENTED PEOPLE

Top people are attracted to a high value.
People are only loyal to the extent that they get what they want.

Will people only stay with you when things are easy?
Most people can stick with you when things go well.

But what will your people do when times are hard?
When you have the right people who possess internal fortitude, they will help you dive into the challenge. When you have weak people, they will run away.

I invite you to ask yourself,

"What do they do when there are struggles?"

"How do you create an inner circle that will create an elite outcome, no matter how hard?"

What would cause a person to leave you in business?
People will leave you for one of these reasons:

1.   They do not receive the benefit/money.
2.   They do not align with the culture.

What qualities should you seek?
Strive to see the best in people. Choose to do your best. Choose to be calm and peaceful.

Speak greatness into others.
The most successful people do not rely on willpower to determine their success.

STANDARDS AND ACCOUNTABILITY

How do you know if you are winning?
If you are running a sales team and intend to win, keep score. If you do not know your performance, you never intentionally will improve.

What is the first step in leading others?
First, define your standards.

If you allow anything below your standards to occur, you have created a new standard because you accept less.

What is the next step to best lead?
After you define your standards, you will meet with your team members one-on-one to understand their goals.

Why do they want to achieve those goals, and what will they do with the money they earn?
It should be clear to all people, including administrative staff, how to earn more money and opportunity.

All the people you lead will have to earn their opportunities. Your job is to stay committed to helping them achieve their intended destination.

Is accountability important?
After you understand what is essential to those you lead, set weekly accountability meetings with them.

These meetings should be no more than thirty minutes.

During the time you meet, you will want to focus on the highest-level activities of **CPI Time** they could do to create the desired outcome.

If a person is not consistently meeting their goals, it will set up the conversation for a very natural transition for them to move away from the role. When this occurs, see if you can find another position on the team they may be better suited for; if none exists, you will have to part ways.

ABOUT TRAINING/COACHING

The best leaders look at their roles as if they are a coach. Therefore, they lead by asking great questions.

What Are Some of the Best Questions for a Leader to Ask?

Some questions to ask include:

- Are we winning?
- What do you think we should do in this situation?
- How can we achieve our goals?
- What is getting in the way?
- How can we move this out of the way?
- How may I help you?
- What do you need from me for you to succeed?

Plan Your Questions Before You Meet

When you meet with your people, know your goal, and keep focused on one question before you move to the next.

Start the meeting where you review the prior week's goals and the progress toward them the person you lead has made. You could ask,

> "Last week, you said you would have two
> first-time appointments, and you had one.

> "What can we do together, so you get three appointments this week to make up for only getting one the prior week?"

What If the Person You Are Leading Reacts Negatively?

Sometimes, if you get an adverse reaction to your leadership, it is probably because the other person is not connecting the dots of how their actions will allow them to achieve their, "Why."

Your job is to help them reconcile this.

> "Bob, you told me you want to take your wife on that great vacation in three months. You said you want to sell one home in addition to the number you normally sell to help you pay for this.
>
> "How can I help you achieve that extra sale to take your vacation?"

How Can You Ask Better Questions?

Ask questions starting with:

- How
- What
- Where
- When

What Questions Should You Avoid?

Unless you are inquiring about why they want to achieve a goal, do not ask questions starting with "Why."

"Why" questions will primarily solicit a defense rather than a solution from the person you lead.

What Is an Example of Using the Strategy Described Above?

Read the examples below and choose which question is more empowering.

Example A:

"Hey Bob, I noticed you haven't hit your goal of taking one listing this week.

"What can you do so that you reach your goal?"

Example B:

"Iley Bob, I noticed that you haven't hit your goal of getting hired by a seller this week.

"So why haven't you taken a listing yet?"

I hope you recognize that Example A is more empowering than Example B.

Dive deep into the conversation to learn what the real opportunity is. Say,

"Tell me more about that."

And then say,

"And what is important to you about that?"

After you set goals, understand what drives your people, and host meetings weekly. Your job is to remove any obstacles to their success.

Your priority is that those on your team are as successful as they can be. Strive to provide those you lead with the necessary training, systems, and support. You might not be in the position to support another with those resources fully, but you should still intend to move toward sharing as much as possible.

People can achieve more than they believe, and when you lead them to think and act to reach what is essential to them, they will often be grateful to you.

Once something is stretched, it does not go back.

- **Role Model**—You demonstrate to another how to do it.
- **Role Play**—They practice with one another.
- **Real Play**—They do it with your guidance.

I inform others about the conversations I will participate in and those I won't. The day-to-day discussions with my teammates and the professional relationships the team builds are aspects I cherish.

How Do I Connect with Those I Lead?

Each team member is seen as an extended family member I guide toward achieving their highest potential.

Most days, every moment of my time is scheduled. Communication is deliberate; I aim to get to the point promptly, which suits some but not all.

My goal is to maximize productivity and value.

What Conversations Should You Hold?

You should consider having the following conversations with your team:

- Acknowledgment of team members' success
- Training
- Development
- Coaching
- Goal setting
- Prospecting
- Prospect conversion
- Writing offers that get accepted
- Negotiating
- Having fun and ideas to promote enjoyment
- Opportunities for improvement in systems or structures
- Proactively avoiding obstacles in a transaction
- Overcoming obstacles as they occur in a sale

What Should You Never Speak About with Those You Lead?

You should never discuss:

- Rumors/gossip
- Other team members with team members in anything less than a positive manner (unless it involves an action that is illegal, unethical, immoral, or harms others or the company; these situations ALWAYS should be brought to leadership's attention ASAP.)
- Lead distribution
- Anything that takes away from the fun, positive, productive environment
- If they ever have a business concern, I ask team members to share it with at least two possible solutions with the appropriate person who can make a difference.

FEEDBACK LOOP

It is crucial to have a feedback loop where you're always thinking about what you've done and how you could do it better.

We embrace End of Day Reports from our inside sales agents and staff. These reports allow us to understand where they perform well and where opportunities for improvement exist.

Once each week, the head of a department touches base with each team member to solicit feedback.

They ask,

- What is the most valuable thing you receive from the team?
- How could the team increase its value to you?
- How could you increase your value to the team?

TEACH TO SELL EXERCISE:

Ask yourself:

- How would you describe a great leader?

____

____

____

- Who was the best leader that helped you?

____

____

____

____

- How do you become a better leader?

____

____

____

____

- Are you a leader or a follower?

____

____

____

- How do you define leadership?

____

____

____

____

CHAPTER SUMMARY: LEAD WITH PURPOSE AND TEACH TO SELL

No matter where you are in your leadership journey, growth comes from action. Purposeful leadership means empowering others to think for themselves and achieve meaningful results.

Key Takeaways

- **Leadership is influence.** It's about empowering others to act and think independently.
- *Teach to Sell* **is a leadership framework** that fosters decision-making and problem-solving skills in others.
- **A great leader meets people where they are** and guides them toward success.
- **True leadership creates impact**—building strong teams and fostering accountability.

- **Success in leadership is measured by how well you help others succeed**; invest in people, and your leadership will grow.
- **Effective leaders remove obstacles.** They focus on solutions, not problems.
- **Leadership requires action**; your next step determines your growth.

Your leadership journey begins with a choice. Will you lead with intention and purpose? The decision is in your hands.

Commit or Quit Challenge: The Leadership Crossroads

You are at a crossroads. You can either step up as a leader and empower others, or you can remain where you are, waiting for leadership to happen to you.

This week, take decisive action:

- Identify one person you can mentor and guide toward success.
- Set up a structured team meeting to foster collaboration and accountability.
- Pinpoint a challenge in your business or team and implement a solution.

Growth happens when you commit to leading with intention. If you hesitate, you risk staying stagnant.

Will you Commit or Quit?

Part V

THE JOURNEY OF
TEACH TO SELL

CHAPTER 13

Embracing the Truth: You Are Good Enough

Throughout my career, I have experienced both victories and setbacks. I have planned, taken action, adjusted course, and at times, hit the mark.

Other times, I have fallen short. But every moment, every challenge, every success, has been a part of my evolution. And through it all, I have learned a truth that took me years to fully accept: **I am good enough.**

Not too long ago, I found myself frustrated with my place in life and business. So, I took a long weekend alone, away from the noise, to reflect. In that solitude, I examined my journey. I looked at where I had been, what I had built, and who I had become.

And what I discovered was this—I had already achieved more than I once believed possible. Of all my accomplishments, what I value most is staying sober, being a devoted dad to my incredible daughter, Maggie, and building a business that has had No Broke Months since 2008.

But my journey has not been without struggle, and I expect neither has yours. The difference between those who thrive and those who remain stuck isn't talent or luck—it's the belief that **you are worthy of success.**

I have learned that within every challenge, there is a lesson waiting to be uncovered. Gratitude allows us to see that truth, and *Teach to Sell* is built on that foundation—the understanding that growth happens when we share, teach, and serve others.

THE LESSONS THAT MATTER

I have done my best to share with you the most valuable lessons I've learned along the way—lessons that extend beyond sales and into life itself. As I reflect, here are the principles that have shaped me the most:

- **Understand your priorities.** Time is finite; where you focus matters.
- **Choose to live with meaning.** Purpose fuels persistence.
- **Develop, learn, and grow.** The greatest investment is in yourself.
- **Understand your worth.** You are capable, and you deserve success.
- **Be committed, not attached, to an outcome.** Adapt when necessary, but never quit.
- **The people you surround yourself with shape your future.** Choose wisely.
- **Pay attention to the right people.** Not everyone is meant to be on your journey.
- **Supplement your weaknesses.** Leverage the strengths of others.
- **Gratitude and negativity cannot coexist.** Choose appreciation over frustration.
- **Focus on one priority at a time.** Progress comes from clarity.
- **Embrace your passion.** It is the driving force behind a fulfilling life.
- *Teach to Sell.* The most powerful way to lead, influence, and create lasting success is by helping others understand, grow, and achieve their own goals.

TEACH TO SELL: A MINDSET, NOT JUST A METHOD

This book has been more than a sales guide; it has been a blueprint for transformation. The principles of *Teach to Sell* go beyond transactions; they are about building trust, creating value, and leading with integrity.

You've learned to educate instead of push, to guide instead of chase, and to connect instead of convince. You've mastered tools like neuro-linguistic programming, the **CPI Communication Model**, and strategic lead generation, all designed to help you serve at the highest level.

But more importantly, you've learned that success is not about what you get—it's about **who you become in the process**.

LIVING THE *TEACH TO SELL* PHILOSOPHY

At the core of *Teach to Sell* is a simple truth: When you teach, you lead. And when you lead, you inspire transformation in others. That transformation begins with you.

Years ago, I decided to leave behind the habits that no longer served me. I committed to growth, integrity, and purpose.

Every morning, I ask myself:

"How may I serve at a higher level today?"

That single question has shaped my journey, through business, fatherhood, and life. It has kept me focused on growth, learning, and making an impact. And now, I pass it on to you.

Ask yourself:

"What action can I take today that will allow
me to create lasting success, not just now, but
ten, twenty years from now?"

You don't have to know every step ahead, but you must decide to show up, teach, and serve today.

The future is not something we wait for. It's something we create.

And so, tomorrow morning, I will wake up and ask again:

"How may I serve at a higher level today?"

I encourage you to do the same.

To your success!

Bibliography

(n.d.). Retrieved from MARS Conference: https://marsconference.com/

Adams, S. (2018, January 15). *The best time of day to schedule a meeting*. Retrieved from Forbes: https://www.forbes.com/sites/susanadams/2018/01/15/the-best-time-of-day-to-schedule-a-meeting

Bandler, R., & Grinder, J. (1975). *Understanding NLP: The Three Principles*. The Structure of Magic I: A Book About Language and Therapy: Science and Behavior Books.

Burdett, E. (2024, November 13). *31 Must-Know Sales Follow-Up Statistics for 2024 Success*. Retrieved from www.peaksalesrecruiting.com/: https://www.peaksalesrecruiting.com/blog/sales-follow-up-statistics/

Chapman Learning Commons. (2024). *Managing your time*. Retrieved from University of British Columbia: https://learningcommons.ubc.ca

Chiarella, T. (2008, August 6). *Just Throw the Damn Ball, Tom Brady*. Retrieved from Esquire: https://www.esquire.com/sports/a4883/tom-brady-0908/

Cialdini, R. B. (2006). *Influence: The psychology of persuasion (Rev. ed.)*. Harper Business.

Couch, D. (2003). *The Warrior Elite: The Forging of SEAL Class 228.* Crown Publishing Group.

Datoo, S. (2019, June 7). *Tips on How to Succeed in Business from Jeff Bezos.* Retrieved from Bloomberg.com: https://www.bloomberg.com/news/articles/2019-06-07/amazon-ceo-jeff-bezos-gives-tips-for-success.

Davidow, M. (2003). Organizational responses to customer complaints: What works and what doesn't. *Journal of Service Research,* 225–250.

Davidow, (2003).

ESPN. (n.d.). *John Wooden's coaching record.* Retrieved from ESPN: https://www.espn.com/nba/story/_/id/10089342/john-wooden-bio

Ferriss, T. (2015, April 15). *Triple H on Pre-Fight Rituals, Injury Avoidance, and Floyd Mayweather, Jr. (#72).* Retrieved from https://tim.blog/: https://tim.blog/2015/04/20/triple-h/

Haig, A. (n.d.).

Heater, B. (2019, January 17). Amazon's MARS Conference to Focus on Machine Learning, Automation, Robotics, and Space. *TechCrunch.*

Herold, B. (2016). *Technology in education: An overview.* Retrieved from Education Week: https://www.edweek.org/technology/technology-in-education-an-overview/2016/02

Howard Schultz: The Man Behind Starbucks' Success. (2018, May 15). *Forbes.*

Keller, G. (2018, August). Mega Agent Camp. (B. Kinney, Interviewer)

Kurzweil, R. (2005). *The Singularity is Near: When Humans Transcend Biology.* Viking Press.

Kurzweil, R. (2005). *The Singularity is Near: When Humans Transcend Biology.* Viking Press.

Lee, B. (1975). *Tao of Jeet Kune Do.* Ohara Publications.

Maclay, K. (2018, January 11). *Social media actually makes you more (not less) relaxed, surprising new research says.* Retrieved from University of California: https://www.universityofcalifornia.edu/news/social-media-actually-makes-you-more-not-less-relaxed-surprising-new-research-says

McCarthy, K. D. (2003). *American Creed: Philanthropy and the Rise of Civil Society 1700-1865.* University of Chicago Press.

McClane, A. J. (1978). *McClane's Field Guide to Saltwater Fishes of North America.* Holt, Rinehart, and Winston.

McNicholas, K. (2013, June 14). *Warren Buffett's former pilot launches Visionary Airlines in Silicon Valley.* Retrieved from Pando: https://pando.com/2013/06/14/warren-buffetts-former-pilot-launches-visionary-airlines-in-silicon-valley/

Mehrabian, A. (1967). *Nonverbal communication.* Aldine Transaction.

Milo, R., & Phillips, R. (2015). *Cell biology by the numbers.* Garland Science.

Morin, A. (2015, October 6). Retrieved from Psychology Today: https://www.psychologytoday.com/us/blog/your-brain-work/201510/10-things-you-dont-know-about-your-brain.

Pfaffmann, C. (n.d). *Human sensory reception*. Retrieved from Encyclopaedia Britannica: https://www.britannica.com/science/human-sensory-reception

Reichheld, F. F., & Sasser, W. (1990). Zero defections: Quality comes to services. *Harvard Business Review*, 105–111.

Richards, C. (2018, December 11). *Warren Buffett's "2-list" strategy: How to maximize your focus and master your priorities*. Retrieved from CNBC: https://www.cnbc.com/2018/12/11/warren-buffetts-2-list-strategy-to-maximize-your-focus-and-priorities.html

Robbins, T. (1991). *Awaken the Giant Within: How to Take Immediate Control of Your Mental, Emotional, Physical and Financial Destiny!* Free Press.

Rosenberg, N. (1994). *Exploring the Black Box: Technology, Economics, and History.* Cambridge University Press.

Sales Stats, Quota and On-Boarding. (2023, August 1). Retrieved from https://channelplaybook.com/: https://channelplaybook.com/telecom/sales-stats-quota-and-on-boarding/

Schaller, R. R. (1997). Moore's law: Past, present and future. *IEEE Spectrum*, 52–59.

Schmidt, C. C. (2007). A time to think: Circadian rhythms in human cognition. *Cognitive Neuropsychology*, 755–789.

Smith, J., & Brown, A. (2020). The Role of Communication in Building Trust: Exploring the Antecedents and Consequences of Trust in a Business Environment. *Harvard Business Review*, 45–67.

Stafford, L. &. (1991). *Maintenance strategies and equity in marriage.* San Diego, CA: Academic Press.

Steve Jobs. (2011). Retrieved from Apple Inc.: https://www.apple.com/newsroom/steve-jobs/

Storm, A. (July, 2 2024). *94 Key Sales Statistics to Help You Sell Smarter in 2024.* Retrieved from https://blog.hubspot.com/: https://blog.hubspot.com/sales/sales-statistics

Thomas, P. (2019, June 28). *Reticular Activating System and Goals | How to Use Your Unconscious Mind to Achieve Your Goals.* Retrieved from Self Help for Life: https://selfhelpforlife.com/reticular-activating-system-and-goals

Tracy, B. (2011). *Eat That Frog!: 21 Great Ways to Stop Procrastinating and Get More Done in Less Time.* Berrett-Koehler Publishers.

Tripp, J. (2015). *NLP and the 3 Principles.* Retrieved from http://hypnosiswithouttrance.com

Trump, D. [. (2016, August 7). Retrieved from twitter: https://twitter.com/realdonaldtrump/status/762369409494646784

Vanden, A. M., Beullens, K., & Roe, K. (2013). Measuring mobile phone use: Gender, age, and real usage level in relation to the accuracy and validity of self-reported mobile phone use. *Mobile Media & Communication*, 213-236.

Walther, J. B. (2005). *Relational aspects of computer-mediated communication: Experimental observations over time.* Organization Science.

Welch, J., & Byrne, J. (2001). *Jack: Straight from the gut.* Warner Books.

Willink, J. (2015). *Discipline equals freedom: Field manual.* St. Martin's Press.

Wooden, J., & Jamison, S. (1997). *Wooden: A lifetime of observations and reflections on and off the court.* McGraw-Hill.

About the Author

DAN ROCHON IS A MASTER of human behavior, influence, and the psychology of success. As a certified practitioner in the art and science of Humanistic Neurolinguistic Psychology and Neuro-Linguistic Programming from the Washington DC Hypnosis Center, he doesn't just understand the human potential—he helps business owners unlock it.

Dan delivers a proven roadmap to consistent and predictable success for entrepreneurs and sales professionals tired of unpredictable income.

Through his *Teach to Sell* methodology, he empowers business owners to eliminate uncertainty, close more deals, and create financial freedom—without gimmicks or guesswork.

Dan doesn't just teach theory; he lives it. Since 2008, he has maintained a flawless track record of no broke months, averaging ten monthly real estate sales—a feat that most agents only dream of.

Dan is the author of *Real Estate Evolution* and *Teach to Sell*, a recognized industry leader, guiding professionals to master influence, avoid costly sales mistakes, and design a business that fuels their ideal life.

His expertise has been featured on *The Nightly News* with Brian Williams, *The Today Show*, CNBC, and *The Washington Post*. As a dynamic keynote speaker, he delivers high-impact strategies that move audiences to action. And with hundreds of thousands of downloads, his *No Broke Months for Salespeople* podcast consistently equips professionals with the tools to win in business and life.

Ready to transform your sales, income, and future? Dan Rochon has the blueprint. The only question is: Are you prepared to execute?